# Microsoft Azure Machine Learning

Explore predictive analytics using step-by-step
tutorials and build models to make prediction in
a jiffy with a few mouse clicks

**Sumit Mund**

BIRMINGHAM - MUMBAI

# Microsoft Azure Machine Learning

First published: June 2015

Production reference: 1100615

Published by Packt Publishing Ltd.
Livery Place
35 Livery Street
Birmingham B3 2PB, UK.

ISBN 978-1-78439-079-2

www.packtpub.com

Cover image by Kamal Kanta Majhi

# Credits

**Author**
Sumit Mund

**Reviewers**
Grigor Aslanyan
Alisson Sol
Abhishek Sur
Radu Tudoran

**Commissioning Editor**
Ashwin Nair

**Acquisition Editor**
Meeta Rajani

**Content Development Editor**
Adrian Raposo

**Technical Editor**
Abhishek R. Kotian

**Copy Editors**
Sonia Michelle Cheema
Neha Vyas

**Project Coordinator**
Sanchita Mandal

**Proofreaders**
Stephen Copestake
Safis Editing

**Indexer**
Monica Ajmera Mehta

**Production Coordinator**
Conidon Miranda

**Cover Work**
Conidon Miranda

# About the Author

**Sumit Mund** is a BI/analytics consultant with about a decade of industry experience. He works in his own company, Mund Consulting Ltd., where he is a director and lead consultant. He is an expert in machine learning, predictive analytics, C#, R, and Python programming; he also has an active interest in Artificial Intelligence. He has extensive experience working with most of Microsoft Data Analytics tools and also on Big Data platforms, such as Hadoop and Spark. He is a Microsoft Certified Solution Expert (MCSE in Business Intelligence).

Sumit regularly engages on social media platforms through his tweets, blogs, and LinkedIn profile, and often gives talks at industry conferences and local user group meetings.

# Acknowledgments

I may have written this book, but this project would never have been a success without the active help and support of many people who have contributed to my journey; I would like to thank them all sincerely and from the bottom of my heart.

Firstly, I'd like to thank the acquisition editor, Meeta Rajani, for approaching and convincing me to write this title. The book improved in manifold ways through valuable comments from all the reviewers, time and again. Adrian Raposo did a commendable job helping develop the content as well as coordinating the overall project management. This book would not have been in its current shape had it not received the perfect touch of the technical editor, Abhishek Kotian, and also all the proofreaders.

Special thanks to my colleagues, Kamal and Mahananda. Kamal took time to get the cover image for the book, while Mahananda took the pain of scanning through the drafts, making sure that all the examples were running well. He also gave suggestions wherever screenshots or steps were changed. When you start writing a book on a product that has been around since its beta days and is still going through changes till its final release, the job of making sure that all the screenshots and steps are correct and up to date is a challenge. Mahananda really made it easy for me.

Last but not least, I'd like to point out that, if someone has suffered because of this project, it's my dear wife, Pallabi. Whether it involved making late night coffee, sacrificing weekends and bank holidays, whenever I implored her to bear with me by saying, "It's the book", she has always responded with a smile, without asking any question. Thank you for all your love, understanding, patience, and support.

I would also like to sincerely thank all those, though not mentioned here, who have helped me in this project directly or indirectly.

# About the Reviewers

**Grigor Aslanyan** is a theoretical cosmologist who mainly focuses on computational methods for data analysis. He has a PhD in physics from the University of California, San Diego, and is currently a postdoctoral research fellow at the University of Auckland in New Zealand.

Grigor was born and raised in Armenia. He obtained his bachelor's and master's degrees in physics and computer science at Yerevan State University, Armenia, before moving to California for his PhD studies. He has also worked as a software engineer for 3 years at Ponté Solutions (which was later acquired by Mentor Graphics).

Grigor's research focuses on studying the theory of the early universe by using experimental data from Cosmic Microwave Background radiation and galaxy surveys. His research requires the development and implementation of complex numerical tools used to analyze the data on large computational clusters, with the ultimate goal of learning about the theory of the early universe. Grigor's current research is focused on applying advanced data science and machine learning techniques to improve the data analysis methods in cosmology, making it possible to analyze large amounts of data expected from current and future generation experiments.

He has implemented the publicly available numerical library, Cosmo++, which includes general mathematical and statistical tools for data analysis as well as cosmology-specific packages. The library is written in C++, and it is publicly available at http://cosmopp.com.

I thank the University of Auckland and my supervisor, Richard Easther, for supporting my work on this book.

**Alisson Sol** is currently a Group Engineering Manager for Microsoft in Bellevue, Washington. He has many years of experience in software development, having hired and managed several software teams that shipped many applications and frameworks, with focus on image processing, computer vision, ERP, business intelligence, big data, machine learning, and distributed systems. Alisson has been working for Microsoft and Microsoft Research in the USA and UK since 2000, and was previously a cofounder of 3 software companies. He has published several technical papers and has several patent applications and granted patents. He has a B.Sc. in physics and an M.Sc. in Computer Science from the Federal University of Minas Gerais, Brazil, and General Management training from the University of Cambridge, UK. When not coding, he likes to play soccer or disassemble hardware, put it back to work, and reuse the spare parts elsewhere!

**Abhishek Sur** has been a Microsoft MVP since 2011. He is currently working as a product head with Insync Tech-Fin Solutions Pvt Ltd. He has profound theoretical insight and years of hands-on experience in different .NET products and languages. Over the years, he has helped developers all over the world through his experience and knowledge. He owns a Microsoft User Group in Kolkata called Kolkata Geeks, and regularly organizes events and seminars in various places to spread .NET awareness. He is a renowned public speaker, voracious reader, and a technology buff. Abhishek's main interest lies in exploring the new realms of .NET technology and coming up with priceless write-ups on the unexplored domains of .NET. He is associated with the Microsoft Insider list on WPF and C# and stays in touch with Product Group teams. He holds a master's degree in computer application along with various other certificates to his credit.

Abhishek is also an author of two books namely, *Visual Studio 2013 and .NET 4.5 Expert Cookbook* and *Visual Studio 2012 and .NET 4.5 Expert Development Cookbook, Packt Publishing*. The books are written on .NET technology with problem - solving approaches and ideals for professionals seeking help for this technology in day-to-day activities.

I would like to acknowledge my wife, Riya, amongst others, for helping me continuously produce this book. You can reach him at books@abhisheksur.com or connect with him through his Twitter handle, @abhi2434.

**Radu Tudoran** obtained his PhD from ENS/IRISA Rennes, France, by working on cloud big data management on a large scale. He obtained his bachelor's degree in engineering and computer science from the Technical University of Cluj-Napoca, Romania, in 2010. Then, he was awarded an ENS Cachan international scholarship for further studies, and he received his master's degree in 2011 from ENS Cachan, France, as well. Next, he received a Matisse scholarship to pursue a PhD. During his PhD studies, he was part of several projects and collaborations with Microsoft, Argonne, Inria Saclay, and Inria Sophia Antipolis. Within the framework of these collaborations, he spent several months at Argonne and Microsoft Research ATL, Europe. His work focuses on providing high-performance services to manage data, batches, or streams within and across cloud data centers. He is the main architect and technical contributor to the A-Brain project on high-performance processing for bioinformatic applications on Azure Cloud, which is in collaboration with Microsoft Research.

# www.PacktPub.com

## Support files, eBooks, discount offers, and more

For support files and downloads related to your book, please visit www.PacktPub.com.

Did you know that Packt offers eBook versions of every book published, with PDF and ePub files available? You can upgrade to the eBook version at www.PacktPub.com and as a print book customer, you are entitled to a discount on the eBook copy. Get in touch with us at service@packtpub.com for more details.

At www.PacktPub.com, you can also read a collection of free technical articles, sign up for a range of free newsletters and receive exclusive discounts and offers on Packt books and eBooks.

https://www2.packtpub.com/books/subscription/packtlib

Do you need instant solutions to your IT questions? PacktLib is Packt's online digital book library. Here, you can search, access, and read Packt's entire library of books.

## Why subscribe?

- Fully searchable across every book published by Packt
- Copy and paste, print, and bookmark content
- On demand and accessible via a web browser

## Free access for Packt account holders

If you have an account with Packt at www.PacktPub.com, you can use this to access PacktLib today and view 9 entirely free books. Simply use your login credentials for immediate access.

## Instant updates on new Packt books

Get notified! Find out when new books are published by following @PacktEnterprise on Twitter or the *Packt Enterprise* Facebook page.

*To my mom, who taught me how to count…*

# Table of Contents

# Preface

You are reading this probably because you are aware of the importance of machine learning and advanced analytics, such as predictive analytics. While there is an increasing demand for people all over the world who possess these skill sets, there is a real scarcity of data scientists who are skilled enough to deliver applications that involve machine learning and advanced analytics and can create real value from the available data.

The reason for this scarcity is because the field of machine learning and data mining used to be the realm of PhDs and experts in subjects such as math, statistics, and programming combined. It's really difficult to find such unicorns. Again, tasks such as predictive analytics have historically been so difficult that even experts, even if they don't exactly struggle, don't find it easy either. This means that years of experience are needed for newcomers to to get on with it.

In this modern age, predictive analytics is on the verge of being industrialized as it is the key to sustaining and promoting the growth of a business. While the scarcity of "unicorn" data scientists doesn't seem to be ending, organizations are now finding solutions to get over this problem. A leading IT research firm, Gartner, suggests that, in the coming days, a new breed of professionals will emerge, referred to as citizen data scientists. Their emergence may bring about such a change that they may soon outnumber unicorn data scientists by a ratio of 5:1.

You might be wondering now, who are these citizen data scientists and where have they come from? They are existing developers, people from the business analyst community, and, possibly, new graduates as well, who are data-savvy, passionate about advanced analytics, and determined to stretch themselves and go in-depth into data science concepts. They will democratize data science and enable the industrialization of advanced analytics.

All this is happening and will continue to happen because of one reason: the arrival of new tools and platforms that make advanced analytics so easy and present data science as a commodity. While this brings huge opportunities for such vendors, it also bring good news for organizations and professionals who are picking it up. There is no doubt that Azure Machine Learning is a leader in this field and Microsoft offers this to organizations, strategically.

Microsoft's corporate vice president, Joseph Sirosh, who is in charge of Azure Machine Learning, describes Azure Machine Learning, as published in CITEworld: "This is the fastest way to build predictive models and deploy them. Very few tools exist today if you're going to build solution on the cloud and create applications. This way you can build intelligent applications from data, then publish as APIs so you can hook them up very easily from any enterprise application—and even from mobile. We're building it simple enough for a high schooler to be able to use it."

This book is an attempt to extend this vision; driven by simplicity, it sets the mission to develop the necessary skills to get started with Microsoft Azure Machine Learning as quickly as possible. The book assumes no prerequisites other than high school math!

# What this book covers

*Chapter 1, Introduction,* sets the context for the book, and it introduces machine learning, predictive analytics, and Azure ML as a whole. It describes a predictive analytics project through its life cycle.

*On your mark: do the background work*

*Chapter 2, ML Studio Inside Out,* explains the ML Studio in detail—the development environment of Azure ML.

*Chapter 3, Data Exploration and Visualization,* familiarizes you with the concepts related to data exploration and visualizations in the first part of this chapter, and then demonstrates the same using ML Studio.

*Chapter 4, Getting Data in and out of ML Studio,* describes the different options available for data input and output inside ML Studio.

*Chapter 5, Data Preparation,* familiarizes you with the different options for data preparation in ML Studio, such as data cleaning, transformation, feature selection, and so on.

*Get Set: build and deploy predictive models*

*Chapter 6, Regression Models*, familiarizes you with the different regression algorithms available, and demonstrates the building of different regression models with step-by-step tutorials.

*Chapter 7, Classification Models*, familiarizes you with the different classification algorithms available and demonstrates the building of different classification models with step-by-step tutorials.

*Chapter 8, Clustering*, explains clustering and then builds a model using ML Studio and the K-means clustering algorithm.

*Chapter 9, A Recommender System*, introduces you to the concepts of a recommendation system and also the options available in ML Studio for you to build your own recommender system. It then walks you through building a recommendation system with a simple example.

*Chapter 10, Extensibility with R and Python*, introduces you to integrating your code in ML Studio using R and Python scripting.

*Chapter 11, Publishing a Model as a Web Service*, explores how easily you can publish a model in an experiment and make it available as a Web service API for others to consume.

*Go: apply your learnings to real-world problems*

*Chapter 12, Case Study Exercise I*, presents a classification problem as a case study exercise.

*Chapter 13, Case Study Exercise II*, presents a regression problem as a case study exercise.

# What you need for this book

To learn and practice the concepts along with the book, you need the following:

- An account in Azure and (ideally) a subscription. You can access the Azure ML service even without a subscription for a few days.
- A browser, Internet Explorer, IE 10, or later versions.
- Lastly, an Internet connection, of course!

# Who this book is for

This book is intended for those who want to learn how to use Azure Machine Learning. Perhaps you already know a bit about machine learning, but have never used ML Studio in Azure, or perhaps, you are an absolute newbie. In either case, this book will get you up and running quickly. Any advanced math, statistics or programming knowledge is not a prerequisite; only high school math is good enough!

# Conventions

In this book, you will find a number of text styles that distinguish between different kinds of information. Here are some examples of these styles and an explanation of their meaning.

Code words in text, database table names, folder names, filenames, file extensions, pathnames, dummy URLs, user input, and Twitter handles are shown as follows: "This means that the `azureml_main` entry point function can import these modules directly."

A block of code is set as follows:

```
def azureml_main(dataframe1 = None, dataframe2 = None):
    #Get all the columns
    cols = dataframe1.columns.tolist()
    #Select columns with name starting with letter 'm'
    dataframe1=dataframe1[[col for col in cols if
    col.startswith('m')]]
    #Return the modified dataset
    return dataframe1
```

**New terms** and **important words** are shown in bold. Words that you see on the screen, for example, in menus or dialog boxes, appear in the text like this: "The **Filter Based Feature Selection** module can identify the most important features in a dataset."

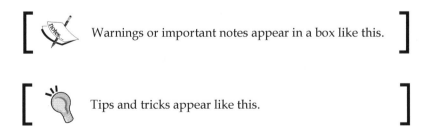

Warnings or important notes appear in a box like this.

Tips and tricks appear like this.

# Reader feedback

Feedback from our readers is always welcome. Let us know what you think about this book—what you liked or disliked. Reader feedback is important for us as it helps us develop titles that you will really get the most out of.

To send us general feedback, simply e-mail feedback@packtpub.com, and mention the book's title in the subject of your message.

If there is a topic that you have expertise in and you are interested in either writing or contributing to a book, see our author guide at www.packtpub.com/authors.

# Customer support

Now that you are the proud owner of a Packt book, we have a number of things to help you to get the most from your purchase.

# Downloading the color images of this book

We also provide you with a PDF file that has color images of the screenshots/ diagrams used in this book. The color images will help you better understand the changes in the output. You can download this file from https://www.packtpub. com/sites/default/files/downloads/Microsoft_Azure_Machine_Learning_ ColorImages.pdf.

# Errata

Although we have taken every care to ensure the accuracy of our content, mistakes do happen. If you find a mistake in one of our books—maybe a mistake in the text or the code—we would be grateful if you could report this to us. By doing so, you can save other readers from frustration and help us improve subsequent versions of this book. If you find any errata, please report them by visiting http://www.packtpub. com/submit-errata, selecting your book, clicking on the **Errata Submission Form** link, and entering the details of your errata. Once your errata are verified, your submission will be accepted and the errata will be uploaded to our website or added to any list of existing errata under the Errata section of that title.

To view the previously submitted errata, go to https://www.packtpub.com/books/ content/support and enter the name of the book in the search field. The required information will appear under the **Errata** section.

# Piracy

Piracy of copyrighted material on the Internet is an ongoing problem across all media. At Packt, we take the protection of our copyright and licenses very seriously. If you come across any illegal copies of our works in any form on the Internet, please provide us with the location address or website name immediately so that we can pursue a remedy.

Please contact us at copyright@packtpub.com with a link to the suspected pirated material.

We appreciate your help in protecting our authors and our ability to bring you valuable content.

# Questions

If you have a problem with any aspect of this book, you can contact us at questions@packtpub.com, and we will do our best to address the problem.

# 1
# Introduction

Welcome to the world of predictive analytics and machine learning! **Azure Machine Learning** enables you to perform predictive analytics with the application of machine learning. Traditionally, it has been an area for experts. Developing and deploying a predictive modeling solution using machine learning has never been simple and easy, even for experts. Microsoft seems to have taken most of the pain out with this new cloud-based offering that allows you to develop and deploy a predictive solution in the simplest and quickest possible way. Even beginners would find it easy and simple to understand.

This chapter, while setting the context for the rest of the book, will present the related topics from a bird's eye view.

## Introduction to predictive analytics

**Predictive analytics** is a niche area of analytics that deals with making predictions of unknown events that may or may not be in future. One example of this would be to predict whether a flight will be delayed or not before the flight takes off. You should not misunderstand that predictive analytics only deals with future events. It can be any concerned event, for example, an event where you need to predict whether a given credit card transaction is a fraud or not when the transaction has already taken place. In this case, the event has already taken place. Similarly, If you are given some properties of soil, and you need to predict a certain other chemical property of soil, then you are actually predicting something that is present.

Predictive Analytics leverages tools and techniques from Mathematics, Statistics, Data Mining and Machine Learning plays a very important role in it. In a typical predictive analytics project, you usually go through different stages in an iterative manner, as depicted in the following figure;

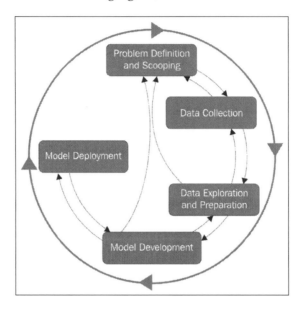

# Problem definition and scoping

In the beginning, you need to understand; what are the business needs and the solutions they are seeking? This may lead you to a solution that lies in predictive analytics. Then, you need to translate the business problem in an analytics problem, for example, the business might be interested in giving a boost to the catalog sales for the existing customers. So, your problem might get translated to predict the number of widgets a customer would buy if you know the demographic information about them, such as their age, gender, income, location, and so on, or the price of an item, given their purchase history of the past several years. While defining the problem, you also need to define the scope of the project; otherwise, it might end up in a never-ending process.

# Data collection

The solution starts with data collection. In some cases, the data may already be there in enterprise storages or in the cloud, that you just have to utilize and in other cases, you need to collect the data from disparate sources. It may also require you to do some **ETL** (**Extract**, **Transform**, and **Load**) work as part of data collection.

# Data exploration and preparation

After you have all the data you need, you can proceed to understand it fully. You do so by data exploration and visualization. This may also involve some statistical analysis.

Data in the real world is often messy. You should always check the data quality and how it fits for your purpose. You have to deal with missing values, improper data, and so on. Again, data may not be present in the proper format, as you would need it to make predictions. So, you may need some preprocessing to get the data in the desired shape. Often, people call it **data wrangling**. After this, you can either select or extract the exact features that lead you to the prediction.

# Model development

After the data is prepared, you choose the algorithm and build a model to make a prediction. This is where machine learning algorithms come in handy. A subset of the prepared data is taken to train the model and then you can choose to test your model with another set or the rest of the prepared data to evaluate its performance. While evaluating the performance, you can try different algorithms and choose the one that performs the best.

# Model deployment

If it is a one-off analysis, you may not bother deploying your trained model. However, often, the prediction made by the model might be used somewhere else. For example, for an e-commerce company, a prediction model might recommend products for a prospective customer visiting the website. In another example, after you have built a model to predict the sales volume for the year, different sales departments across different locations might need to use it to make the forecasts for their region. In such scenarios, you have to deploy your trained model as a web service or in some other type of production, so that others can consume it either by a custom application, **Microsoft Excel**, or a similar tool.

For most of the practical cases, these phases never remain in isolation and are always worked on in an iterative manner.

This book, with an overview of the different common options available for data exploration and preparation, focuses on model development and deployment. In fact, model development and deployment is the core offering of Azure Machine Learning with the limited options for data exploration and preparation. You can make use of other Azure services, such as **HDInsight**, **Azure SQL Database**, and so on, or programming languages outside it for the same.

# Machine learning

Samuel Arthur, known to be the father of machine learning, defines it as a field of study that gives computers the ability to learn without being explicitly programmed. To simplify it, machine learning is a scientific discipline that explores the construction and study of algorithms that can learn from data. Such algorithms operate by building a model from example inputs and use that model to make predictions or decisions rather than following strictly static program instructions.

To illustrate, consider that you have a dataset that contains the information about age, education, gender, and annual income of a sufficiently large number of people. Suppose you are interested in predicting someone's income. So, you will build a model by choosing a machine learning algorithm and train the model with the dataset. After you train your model, it can then predict the income of a new person if you provide it with age, education, and gender data. To explain it further, you have not programmed something explicitly, such as if a male's age is greater than 50 and whether he has a master's degree, then he would earn say $100,000 per annum. However, what you did was just choose a generic algorithm and gave it the data, so that it discovers all the relationships between the different variables or features (here, age, gender, and education) with the target variable income. So, the algorithm learned from the data and hence got trained. Now, with the trained algorithm, you can predict someone's income if you know their other variables.

The preceding example is a typical kind of machine learning problem where there exists a target variable or class; here that is income. So, the algorithm learns from the training data or examples and then after being trained, the algorithm predicts for a new case or data point. Such learning is known as the **Supervised Machine Learning**. It works as shown in the following figure:

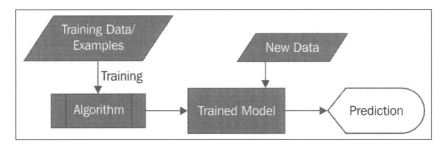

There is another kind of machine learning where there is no target variable or the concept of training data or examples, so here, the prediction is also of a different kind. Consider the same dataset again that contains data of age, gender, education, and income of a sufficiently large number of people. You have to run a targeted marketing campaign, so you have to divide or group the people into three clusters. In this case as well, you can use a different kind of machine learning generic algorithm on the dataset that would automatically group the people into three groups or clusters. This kind of machine learning is known as **unsupervised machine learning**.

There is also another kind of machine learning that makes recommendations; remember how Amazon recommends books or Netflix recommends movies—which might surprise you as to how magically they know about a user's choice or taste.

Though machine learning is not limited to these three kinds, for the scope of this book, we would limit it to these three.

Again, the scope of this book and, of course, Azure Machine Learning limits the application of machine learning to just the area of predictive analytics only. You should be aware that machine learning is not limited to this. Machine learning finds it roots in artificial intelligence and powers a variety of applications, some of which you use in everyday life, for example, web search engines, such as Bing or Google are powered by Machine Learning or applications, so also personal digital assistants like Microsoft's Cortana and Apple's Siri. These days, driverless cars are also in the news, which use machine learning. So, such applications are countless.

# Types of machine learning problems

The following are some of the common kinds of problems solved through machine learning.

## Classification

**Classification** is the kind of machine learning problem where inputs are divided into two or more classes and the learner produces a model that assigns unknown inputs to one (or multi-label classification) or more of these classes or labels. This is typically handled in a supervised way. Spam detection is an example of classification, where the inputs or examples are e-mail (or other) messages and the classes are "spam" and "not spam" and the model to predict a new e-mail as spam or not are based on example data.

# Regression

**Regression** problems involve predicting a numerical or continuous value for the target variable for the new data given in the dataset with one or more features or dependent variables and associated target values. A simple example can be where you have historical data of the price paid for different properties in your locality for say the last 5 years. Here, the price paid is the target variable and the different attributes of a property, such as the total built-up area; the type of property, such as a flat or semi-detached house; and so on, are different features or variables. A regression problem would be to predict the property price of a new property available in the market for sale.

# Clustering

**Clustering** is an unsupervised learning problem and works on a dataset with no label or class variable. This kind of algorithm takes all of the data and groups them into different clusters say 1, 2, and 3, which were not known previously. The clustering problem is fundamentally different from the classification problem. The classification problem is a supervised learning problem where your class or target variable is known to train a dataset, whereas in clustering, there is no concept of label and training data. It works on all the data, and groups them into different clusters.

So, to put it simply, if you have a dataset and a class/label or target variable as a categorical variable, and you have to predict the target variable for a new dataset based on the given dataset (example), then this is a classification problem. If you are just given a dataset with no label or target variable and you just have to group them into $n$ clusters, then it's a clustering case.

# Common machine learning techniques/ algorithms

The following are some of the very popular machine learning algorithms:

# Linear regression

**Linear regression** is probably the most popular and classic statistical technique used for regression problems to make prediction for a continuous value from one or more variables or features. This algorithm uses a linear function and it optimizes the coefficients that fit best to the training data. If you have only one variable, then you may think of this model as a straight line that best fits the data. For more features, this algorithm optimizes best hyperplane that fits the training data.

# Logistic regression

**Logistic regression** is a statistical technique used for classification problems. It models the relationship between a dependent variable or a class label and independent variables (features) and then makes a prediction of a categorical dependent variable or a class label. You may think of this algorithm as a linear regression for a classification problem.

# Decision tree-based ensemble models

A **decision tree** is a set of questions or decisions and their possible consequences arranged in a hierarchical fission. While the plain decision tree is not very powerful, an assembly of trees with the averaged out results can be very effective. These are ensemble models and differ by how the decision is sampled or chosen. **Random forest** or **decision forest** and **boosted decision tree** are two very popular and powerful algorithms. Decision tree-based algorithms can be used for both classification and regression problems.

# Neural networks and deep learning

**Neural networks** algorithms are inspired by how a human brain works. It builds a network of computation units, neurons, or nodes. In a typical network, there are three layers of nodes: first, the input layer, the middle layer or hidden layer, and in the end, the output layers. Neural networks algorithms can be used for both classification and regression problems.

A special kind of neural networks algorithms where there are more than three layers along with the input and output layers and more than one hidden layers are known as **Deep learning** algorithms. These are getting increasingly popular these days because of remarkable results.

Though Azure Machine Learning is capable of deep learning (convolutional neural network—a flavor of the deep learning model as of writing of this book), the book does not include it.

# Introduction to Azure Machine Learning

Microsoft Azure Machine Learning or in short Azure ML is a complete cloud service. It is accessible through the browser Internet Explorer (IE) 10 or its later versions. This means that you don't need to buy any hardware or software and don't need to worry about deployment and maintenance.

So, it's a fully managed cloud service that enables analysts, data scientists, and developers to build, test, and deploy predictive analytics into their applications or in a standalone analysis. It turns machine learning into a service in the easiest possible way and lets you build a model visually through drag and drop. Azure ML helps you to gain insight even of massive datasets, bringing all the benefits of the cloud by integrating other big data that processes an Azure service such as HDInsight (Hadoop) to machine learning.

Azure ML is powered by a decent set of machine learning algorithms. Microsoft claims that these are state-of-the-art algorithms coming from Microsoft Research and some of these actually power flagship products, such as Bing search, Xbox, Cortana, and so on.

# ML Studio

Azure Machine Learning Studio or in short ML Studio is the development environment for Azure ML. It's totally browser-based and hence is accessible from a modern browser, such as IE 10 or its later versions. It also provides a collaborative environment where you can share your work with others.

ML Studio provides a visual workspace to build, test, and iterate on a predictive model easily and interactively. You create a workspace and create experiments inside it. You can consider making an experiment inside ML Studio as a project where you drag and drop datasets and analysis modules onto an interactive canvas, connecting them together to form a predictive model. Usually, you iterate your model's design, edit the experiment, save a copy if desired, and run it again. When you're ready, you can publish your experiment as a web service, so that it can be accessed by others or other applications.

When your requirement can't be met visually by dragging and dropping modules, ML Studio allows you to extend your experiment by writing code in either R or Python scripting. It also provides you a module that allows you to play with data using SQL queries.

# Summary

You just finished the first chapter, which not only introduces you to predictive analytics, machine learning, and Azure ML, but also sets the context for the rest of the book. You started by exploring predictive analytics and learned about the different stages for a typical predictive analytics task. You then moved on to a high-level understanding of machine learning by gaining some knowledge about it. You also learned about the common type of problems solved through machine learning and some of the popular algorithms. After that, you got a very high-level overview of Azure ML and ML Studio.

The next chapter is all about ML Studio. It introduces you to the development environment of Azure ML with an overview of the different components of ML Studio.

# 2
# ML Studio Inside Out

While working on a predictive analysis model, you typically follow different steps, such as pulling data from one or more sources, exploring and preparing data, or applying different algorithms to get your desired output. Then, you test and improve on it. Usually, this is an iterative process. Once you are happy with your model, you find ways so that it can be deployed for production and other people or applications can consume or make use of your developed model.

To perform the preceding tasks, you need an environment with the right tools available. ML Studio provides you with everything to develop and deploy a predictive model.

In this chapter, you will start exploring ML Studio after you know how to create a Microsoft account and a Azure ML workspace. Then, you will get introduced to different parts of ML Studio and learn how to create an experiment. You can also find out, briefly, how to work with other projects in ML Studio collaboratively. This chapter aims to familiarize you with the environment without doing any actual work, which is the content for the chapters following this one.

## Introduction to ML Studio

ML Studio gives you an interactive visual workspace to easily build, test, and iterate a predictive analysis model.

You drag-and-drop datasets and analysis modules onto an interactive canvas, connecting them together to form an experiment, which you submit to ML Studio to run or execute. To iterate your model design, you edit the experiment, save a copy if desired, and submit it again.

There is no programming required for this; visually connecting datasets and modules to construct your predictive analysis model is enough. However, if you need more functionality than what is available visually in ML Studio out of the box, you can write **R** or **Python** code to get the desired result. R or Python programming is not an absolute must to work with ML Studio.

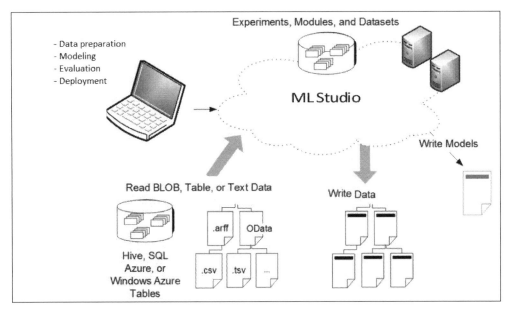

https://azure.microsoft.com/en-gb/documentation/articles/machine-learning-what-is-ml-studio/

Before you start working with ML Studio, you need to get a subscription for Microsoft Azure and sign in to ML Studio. The following section walks you through the process if you are not familiar with it.

# Getting started with Microsoft Azure

Getting into the details of **Microsoft Azure** is beyond the scope of this book. However, the following subsection details the steps to start with it by creating an account and starting a subscription.

# Microsoft account and subscription

If you don't already have a Microsoft account, you need to create one by visiting `http://www.microsoft.com/account`. This URL might change in future and if so, you can just search online for **Microsoft Account** to find the right URL.

At the time of writing this book, if you sign up for the first time, Microsoft offers you a free trial for a month and a credit worth $200 to spend on the services on Azure, which is more than enough if you just need to follow through the examples in this book and use only ML Studio.

Once you are successfully signed in, you can visit https://manage.windowsazure.com/ to find different services available through Azure.

# Creating and managing ML workspaces

You can scroll through on the left-hand side of the Azure services panel and click on **Machine Learning**.

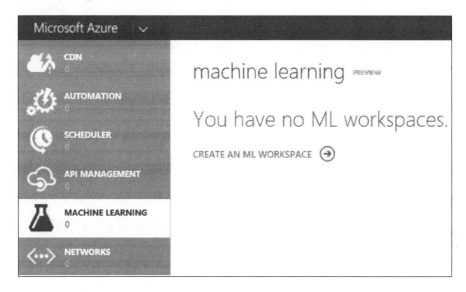

To create a project in machine learning follow the steps:

1. Click on the **CREATE AN ML WORKSPACE** option.
2. In the **QUICK CREATE** page, enter your workspace information.

> Note that the **WORKSPACE OWNER** option is your Microsoft account (name@outlook.com) or organization account.

3. Click on the **CREATE AN ML WORKSPACE** option.

4. After your ML workspace is created, you will see it listed on the machine learning page, as shown in the following screenshot:

You can create more than one workspace and manage them all from this area. Click on the created workspace and it will take you to its dashboard page where you can also find the option to configure it. Then, click on the **OPEN IN STUDIO** link to enter in ML Studio.

You can also go straight to ML Studio using `https://studio.azureml.net/home`.

# Inside ML Studio

You usually land at the ML Studio home page that contains a bunch of links to different resources, including documentation and quick-start videos.

Apart from ML Studio Home, you will also find the following tabs on the left-hand side of the screen:

- **EXPERIMENTS**: These are the experiments that have been created, run, and saved
- **WEB SERVICES**: This is a list of experiments that you have published

- **DATASETS**: This is a collection of all the datasets that are either uploaded or saved from a experiment along with all the sample ones
- **TRAINED MODELS**: This is a list of all the trained models
- **SETTINGS**: This is a collection of settings that you can use to configure your account and resources

# Experiments

You can think of an experiment as any analysis you would perform in ML Studio — it can be a simple one, such as a simple statistical analysis, or a complex predictive analysis. An experiment inside ML Studio is a collection of modules connected hierarchically. A module is a unit that encapsulates a machine learning library provided in ML Studio and performs a task common in machine learning scenarios. A dataset after it is uploaded to ML Studio is also available as a module to be used in an experiment. You just need to drag a module to the canvas of the experiment and visually join the output port of one to the input port of another to build the workflow for your model. A module may have one or more input ports or no input port at all. However, it must have at least one output port. You may think of a module as a block that may take inputs and generate a dataset per output port as output.

You can create more than one experiment in a workspace.

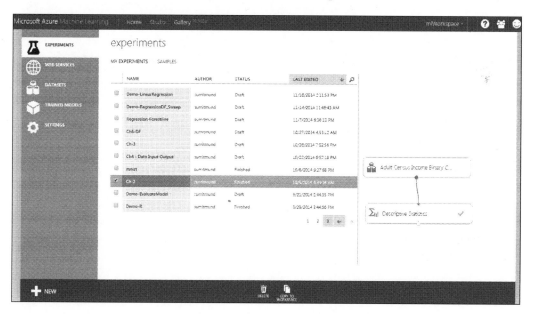

# Creating and editing an experiment

To create a new experiment, click on the **+ NEW** button at the bottom of the left-hand side of the screen and then choose **Blank Experiment**. A new experiment will appear.

When you create a new experiment, you will see the following view. The interface includes a module palette, an experiment canvas, a properties panel, and various menus and controls at the top, bottom, and far left of the screen.

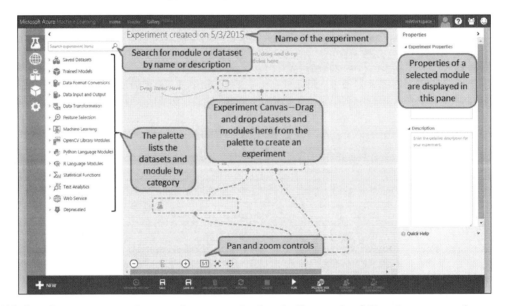

While editing an experiment, the screen looks similar to the following screenshot. Clicking on a module displays its parameters in the properties pane to the right of the experiment canvas—you can view and modify parameters in this pane.

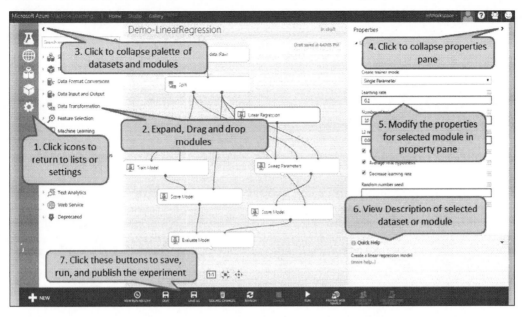

To check the various options that are present on the screen, follow the steps:

1. Click on the icons on the screen to return to lists or settings.

2. Expand drag and drop.

3. Click on the < icon to collapse the palette of datasets and modules as shown in the preceding screenshot.

4. Click on the > icon to collapse the properties pane as shown in the preceding screenshot.

5. Modify the properties for the selected module in the property pane.

6. View the description of the selected dataset or module.

7. Click on these buttons to save, run, and publish the experiment.

To zoom and pan the experiment canvas, you can use the controls at the bottom of the page.

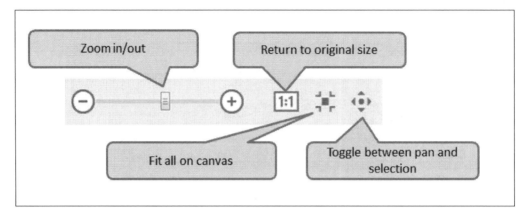

The slider bar to the left zooms the experiment canvas in and out. You can click on the - and + buttons or use the mouse to slide the bar to left and right.

Click on the **1:1** button to return the experiment to its actual size; you can also type *9* on the keyboard to do so. The button to the right of the **1:1** button zooms the experiment to fit on the canvas; you can also type *0* on the keyboard to do so.

# Running an experiment

When you click on the **RUN** button below the experiment canvas, the experiment is submitted to ML Studio to be executed.

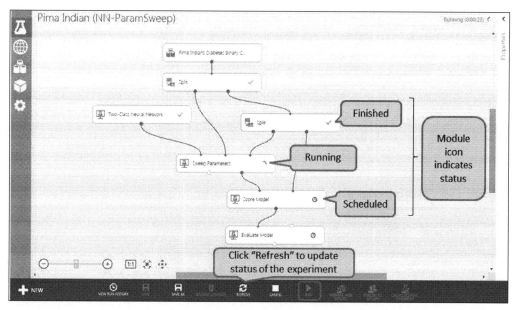

After submitting an experiment, you can click on the **REFRESH** button below the experiment canvas to update the status of each module as the experiment gets executed. Status icons on the modules indicate the status information of the modules (datasets do not display a status indicator). Let's take a look at the following table:

| clock | ⏰ | This icon tells you that the module is scheduled to run |
|---|---|---|
| **busy indicator** | ↻ | This icon indicates that the module is running |
| **green check mark** | ✓ | This icon means that the module ran successfully |
| **red X** | ⊗ | This icon indicates that the module has encountered an error |

An experiment is completed once all the modules display green check marks, indicating that all modules are executed successfully, or when a module displays a red X, indicating that it has failed. If a module fails, the experiment terminates and other modules in the experiment may not get executed.

You are able to view the results of any module in an experiment once it has executed. To do so, right-click on the output port of a module and select the **Visualize** option. You may view the output of a module or save the output as a dataset for use in other experiments. If you save it, then it would be available as a saved dataset in ML Studio.

If a module fails, there are logs that you can examine. These logs can be helpful to include in bug reports to Microsoft. Links to the output and error logs can be found in the properties pane when you select the module. You can also access them by right-clicking on the module and selecting the **View Log** option.

After an experiment has run, you can modify it and run it again. After editing an experiment, you can click on the **SAVE** button below the experiment canvas to save your work or you can click on the **SAVE AS** option to save a copy of the experiment under a different name. When you are ready to run the experiment again, click on the **RUN** option. Each copy of the experiment that you save or run is listed in the **EXPERIMENTS** list in the ML Studio default view.

## Creating and running an experiment – do it yourself

Now that you know enough about an experiment, lets create and run a simple experiment:

1. Create a new experiment by clicking on the **+ NEW** button at the bottom of the left-hand side of the screen and then choose the **Black Experiment** option.

2. On the canvas of the new experiment, name the new project as **Ch-2**.

3. Expand the **Saved Datasets** modules to the left of the screen and drag the first dataset named **Adult Census Income Binary Classification dataset** and drop it in to the center of the canvas.

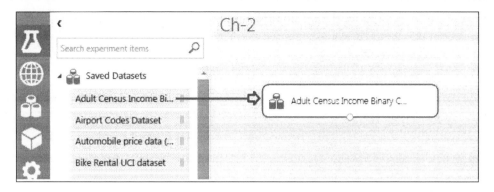

4.  Collapse the **Saved Datasets** modules and expand the **Statistical Functions** modules. Then, drag the **Descriptive Statistics** module to the canvas.

5.  Connect the output port of the **Adult Census Income Binary Classification dataset** module to the input port of the **Descriptive Statistics** module.

6.  Click on the **RUN** button at the bottom of the screen. It should run without any error marking the **Descriptive Statistics** module with a green tick mark, as shown in the following screenshot:

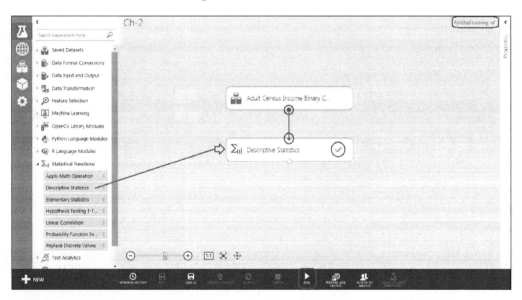

After running the experiment, it already gets autosaved. You may exit from the workspace now. At this point, we are not concerned about investigating the result of the experiment, which you will learn in the subsequent chapters.

# Workspace as a collaborative environment

Workspaces enable groups to work on common projects by gathering data, modules, and experiments together in a single location for common use. Workspaces let users securely share ideas and resources. You can be a member of several workspaces and can easily switch between them.

As the owner of a workspace, you can invite others to the workspace by clicking on the **Setting** icon on the left-hand side of the screen and then clicking on **USERS** from the top tabs. You can invite others to the workspace by adding their Microsoft accounts.

Once you have successfully added other users, they can use the same workspace like you as an owner can, except that they can't invite others unless you give them ownership privileges.

One user can be an owner or user of more than one workspace.

 Note that a workspace can be shared and owned by multiple users, but billing is made only to the user who created the workspace.

# Summary

Practically speaking, ML Studio is the *Microsoft Azure Machine Learning*! If you are working on a predictive analysis, ML Studio provides a platform for everything—for development, testing and deployment. It does this in the easiest way possible, just by mouse clicks.

In this chapter, you started with creating a Microsoft account and creating an ML workspace. Then, you explored ML studio from inside out. You moved on to create a simple experiment in ML Studio and also quickly explored how ML Studio can be used as a collaboration environment to work with others.

Now that you know ML Studio, in the next chapter you will learn about data exploration and data visualization using ML Studio.

# 3
# Data Exploration and Visualization

Before you do any analysis and find results from your dataset, you need to understand the data. You can do so by data exploration and visualization. ML Studio provides a very basic option to do so, but with the most essential information. To use the tool and understand the data, you need to be familiar with some of the basic concepts such as **mean**, **standard deviation**, **variables**, or **features** in a dataset, and basic plotting techniques, such as **histogram**, **box plot**, **scatter plot**, and so on. The first part of this chapter will familiarize you with these concepts and then you will find the use of these inside ML Studio to apply them to a sample dataset. If you are a practitioner or are familiar with statistics, feel free to skip the basic concepts section and move on to the next.

# The basic concepts

The following is a very simple dataset with four features or variables: name, age, gender, and monthly income in dollars ($). A dataset may also be known as a set of observations. The term's features and variables are used interchangeably in most places and also in this book. Let's take a look at the following table:

<-----------------Features ---------->

| Name | Age | Gender | Monthly Income($) |
|---|---|---|---|
| Person A | 20 | Male | 2000 |
| Person B | 45 | Female | 5000 |
| Person C | 36 | Male | 3000 |
| Person D | 55 | Male | 6500 |
| Person E | 27 | Female | 2800 |
| Person F | 31 | Male | 5900 |
| Person G | 33 | Male | 4800 |
| Person X | 59 | Female | 2400 |
| Person Y | 42 | Male | 7200 |
| Person Z | 29 | Female | 3100 |

Rows or records in the dataset are also known as examples in the machine learning context. There are 10 examples in this dataset. Here, the **Name** column represents the unit of observation—the unit described by the data that one analyzes. So, you may say that **Person A** has the features: 20, Male, and 2000.

A feature can be numeric or categorical. A numeric feature contains numeric values, such as **Age** and **Monthly Income($)** in this case. You can apply mathematical operations to a numeric feature. A categorical feature usually contains string values for a set of categories. For example, **Gender** can be of two categories, as in this dataset—**Male** or **Female**. In some cases, a categorical feature can also assume values that are numeric, for example, you may like to represent **Male** with the number **0** and **Female** with **1**. So, the feature **Gender** will have values 0 and 1, but it will still be a categorical feature or variable.

# The mean

The mean is the average of numbers. It is simple to calculate: add up all the numbers and then divide by how many numbers there are. In other words, it is the sum divided by the count.

For example, the mean of the five values: 5, 18, 37, 20, and 85 is:

$$\frac{5+18+37+20+85}{5} = \frac{165}{5} = 33$$

Now to get more formal, you can express the mean, the arithmetic mean, of a sample as:

$$x_1, x_2, ..., x_n$$

It is the sum of the sampled values divided by the number of items in the sample: $\mu$

$$Mean, \mu\left(pronounced\ as\ mu\right) = \frac{x_1 + x_2 + ... + x_n}{n}$$

Now, you can find out what the mean of age in the dataset is (refer to table 3.1).

$$\frac{20+45+36+55+27+31+33+69+42+29}{10} = \frac{377}{10} = 37.7$$

# The median

The median is the middle number in a sorted list of numbers. If you have the numbers: 5, 18, 37, 20, and 85. To find the median, sort them in the ascending order: 5, 18, **20**, 37, and 85. As you can find out, the middle number is in position 3, where there are 5 numbers. The median here is 20.

In a set of numbers where the count is even, say 10, the median will be average of the middle two numbers, so at the position of 5 and 6.

Now, you can find out what is the median of the age variable in the dataset (refer to table 3.1). Sort them in the following order:

20, 27, 29, 31, **33**, **36**, 42, 45, 55, and 59

The median here can be calculated as *(33 + 36)/2 = 69/2 = 34.5.*

# Standard deviation and variance

Standard deviation is the square root of variance. It is usually represented by the Greek letter sigma, σ, and the variance is represented as σ2. You may be wondering now, how the variance, or σ2, is calculated. It is the average of the squared differences from the mean. The following figures provide the mathematical formula for calculating variance and standard deviation:

$$Variance, \sigma^2 = \frac{1}{n}\sum_{i=1}^{n}(x_i - \mu)^2$$

$$Standard\ Deviation, \sigma = \sqrt{\frac{1}{n}\sum_{i=1}^{n}(x_i - \mu)^2}$$

If you calculate the standard deviation for the age variable in the dataset (refer to table 3.1), you will find the answer to be 12.4637.

Variance and standard deviation explain how the data is spread around the mean. When variance is large, it shows that data is spread more widely around the mean. The standard deviation shows that on an average, how much a value differs from the mean. So, in the dataset (refer to table 3.1), each value on an average differs by 12.4637 from the mean, which is 37.7.

Putting it all together for the dataset, ML studio can show you the following statistics:

| | Name | Age | Gender | Monthly-Income($) |
|---|---|---|---|---|
| Mean | | 37.7 | | 4270 |
| Median | | 34.5 | | 3950 |
| Min | | 20 | | 2000 |
| Max | | 59 | | 7200 |
| Standard Deviation | | 12.4637 | | 1850.5555 |
| Unique Values | 10 | 10 | 2 | 10 |
| Missing Values | 0 | 0 | 0 | 0 |
| Feature Type | String | Numeric | String | Numeric |

Note that, here **Min** means the minimum value and **Max** means the maximum value. So, the maximum monthly income is 7200 where the minimum age is 20. The **Unique Values** variable shows how many unique values there are for that feature, for example, for **Gender**, there are two: male and female. The **Missing Values** variable identifies the number of cases where the value is not present for a feature. Though it is included here, the unit of observation is not included (referred to here as **Name**) during analysis.

# Understanding a histogram

A histogram visually shows how data is distributed using bars of different heights. You may consider the dataset (refer to table 3.1) and say you are interested in knowing how age is distributed. You can split all the ages in two groups or two bins. Let's take a look at the following table:

| Age group | No of people |
| --- | --- |
| 20 to 39.5 | 6 |
| 39.5 to 59 | 4 |

So, you will have the histogram for age with two bins, shown as follows:

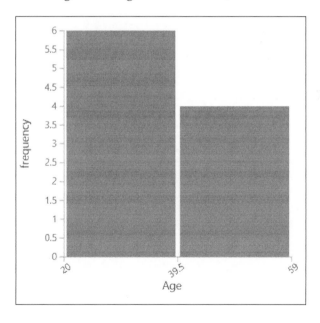

Similarly, the histogram for Monthly Income (refer to table 3.1) with five bins would look something like as shown in the following graph:

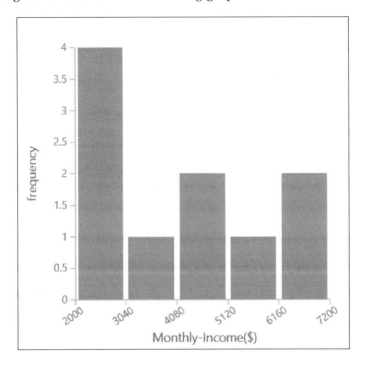

# The box and whiskers plot

The **Box** plot is another way to graphically show how the data is distributed. It shows three quartiles of data, Q1, Q2 and Q3 at the bottom, middle, and top of the box, respectively. Considering the dataset from table 3.1, the quartile values will be as follows:

- *Q1 = 25th percentile = 29.5*
- *Q2 = Median (50th percentile) = 34.5*
- *Q3 = 75th percentile = 44.25*

Based on these values, the IQR (Interquartile Range) can be calculated as *Q3 – Q1* and the Lower Boundary or Lower Whisker can be calculated as *Q1 – 1.5 \* IQR*.

If the Min value is greater than *Q1 – 1.5 \* IQR*, then *Lower Boundary or Lower Whisker = min value*. So, for our example, we are considering the *Upper Boundary or Upper Whisker = 20*

*Upper Boundary or Upper Whisker = Q3 + 1.5 \* IQR*

If the Max value is less than *Q3 + 1.5 \* IQR*, then *Upper Boundary or Upper Whisker = max value*. For our example, we are considering *Upper Boundary or Upper Whisker = 59*.

Let's take a look at the following diagram:

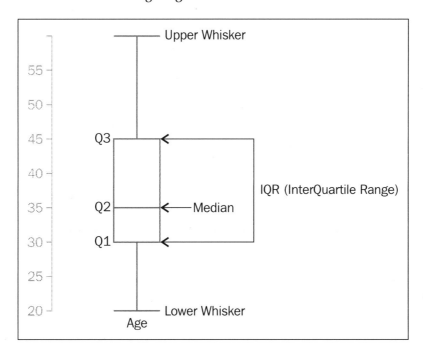

In a box and whiskers plot, if for any quartile the distance is short, then the data is bunched in that region and when the distance is longer, it signifies that the data is more spread out for that region. In the preceding plot, Q2 is the shortest, which means that the data points are more compact in that quartile, whereas Q4 is longer, which indicates that the data points have been spread out.

# The outliers

Any value that falls outside the lower or upper whiskers is known as an outlier. On a plot, these are represented as simple dots, as shown in the following diagram:

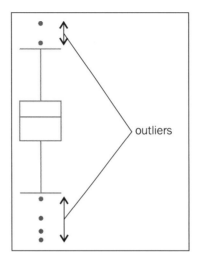

# A scatter plot

A **scatter** plot is a graphical representation of two sets of variables. The data is displayed as a collection of points on a 2D space with one variable projected on the *x* axis and another on the *y* axis. The following is a scatter plot with Age on the *x* axis and Monthly-Income on the *y* axis (refer to the dataset in table 3.1):

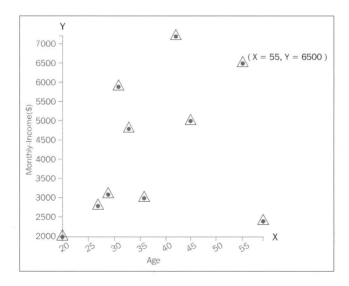

For the sake of illustration, we have labeled one point of $x$ axis as *55* and one point of $y$ axis as *6500*. So this represents the values of Age and Monthly-Income on the 2D space. If you draw a perpendicular line vertically from the point to the $x$ axis, it would touch 55 and if you draw a perpendicular line horizontally from the point on $y$ axis, it would touch 6500.

A scatter plot visually shows the relationship between two sets of data.

# Data exploration in ML Studio

Now, it's time to apply these concepts and start with data exploration and visualization using ML Studio. You will use some of the sample datasets, which comes by default, and do some basic exploration.

# Visualizing an automobile price dataset

The **Automobile price data (Raw)** module is available on the left-hand side modules palette under **Saved Datasets**. This dataset is about automobiles distinguished by their make and model, including the price and features, such as the number of cylinders and MPG and an insurance risk score known to actuaries as symboling. If symboling has a value of +3, this indicates that the auto is risky and a value of -3 indicates that it is probably pretty safe.

Expand the **Saved Datasets** section in the modules palette. Drag the **Automobile price data (Raw)** module to the canvas. To get the visualized graph of the data, follow the steps:

1. Right-click on the output port.
2. Click on **Visualize**.

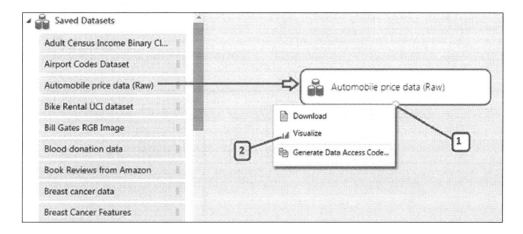

The visualization window will be displayed as a popup:

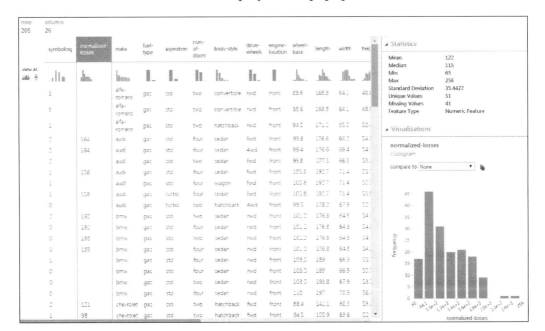

You can find the following information in the visualization window:

- The total number of rows and columns are 205 rows and 26 columns.

- It displays the first 100 rows of data.

- In the Statistics Area, when you click on any column, it would display the basic statistics on the right-hand side of the screen: the mean, median, minimum value, maximum standard deviation value, number of unique values, and number of missing values. It also shows the feature type of the selected column.

- In the Visualizations Area, at the bottom right-hand side of the screen is the graph area for the selected feature. Click anywhere on the feature column to see the graph for that column.

# A histogram

Any feature whether numeric or string can be displayed as a histogram. It is the default graph that appears on the screen. On the visualization window, click on the **drive-wheels** column and you can find the following histogram:

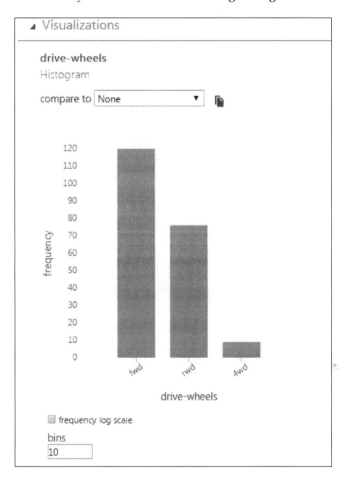

When you click on a numeric variable, such as price, you will find the following graph:

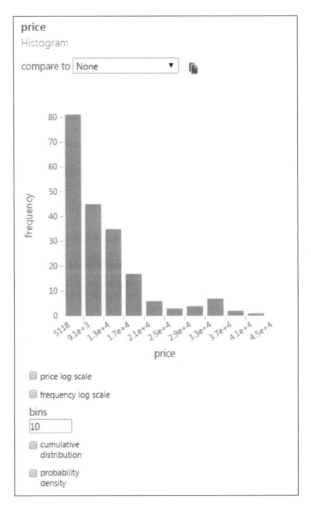

The price value in the preceding graph appears in a scientific notation, but if you hover your cursor on any one, you can see the actual value as a tooltip. For example, if you hover your mouse cursor on *1.3e+4*, you would see the value *13174.4*.

In the graph, the bin size is set to the default value of 10. However, you can change it to make more sense of the graph. In the previous graph, change the bins to **20** and press *Tab* on the keyboard to find the changed graph.

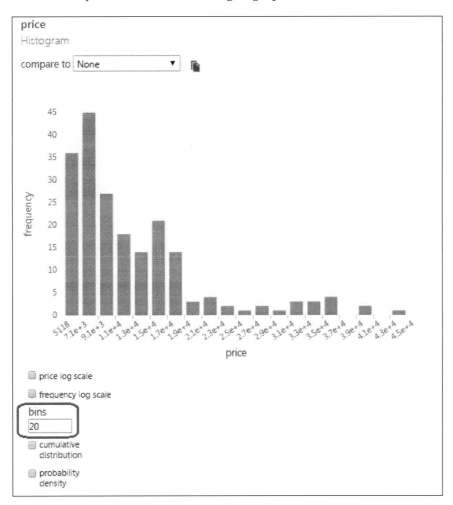

When there is large range of values, sometimes, the log scale is used so that they can be better represented. Click on the checkbox for **price log scale** to find the following modified graph:

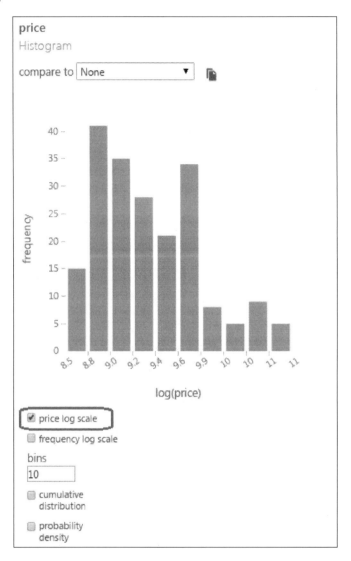

# The box and whiskers plot

While histogram can be made from both numerical and string variables, a box plot can only be made from numerical variables. When you click on the little icon of the box plot in the view as section, you can see all the columns that can be represented as a box and whiskers plot on the top columns in the visualization window.

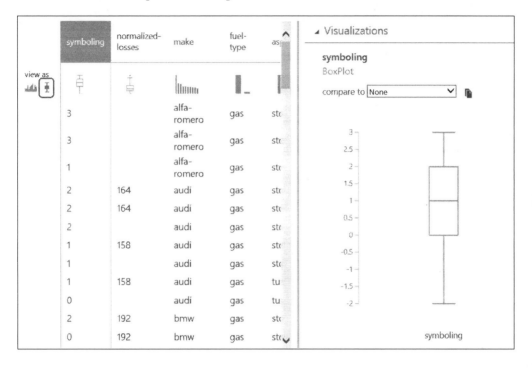

Now, click on **price column** and notice the outliers in the box plot, as shown in the following screenshot:

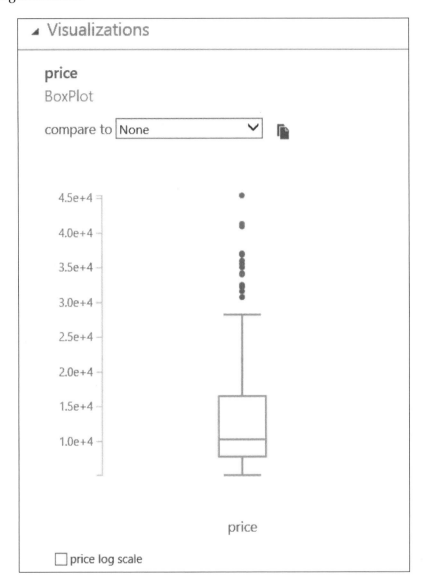

# Comparing features

You can select one feature and compare it with another feature. If both the features are numeric (and are not marked as a label), then the comparison is displayed as a scatter plot. If either of the features is nonnumeric (string), then the comparison is displayed as a box plot.

Click on the **price** section and then select **make** from the **compare to** drop-down list in the graph area. Note how the price is distributed for different manufacturers in the graph. The **make** column contains the name of different manufacturers.

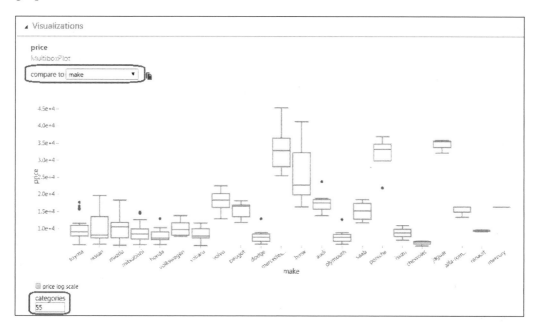

Now, you may try comparing two numerical features. Select the **price** column and then compare it to **normalized-losses**.

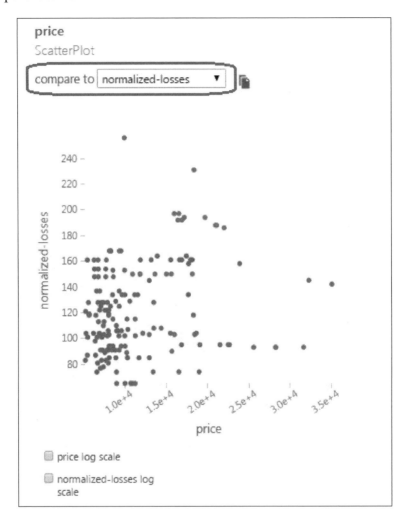

# A snapshot

You can create a snapshot of a graph by clicking on the snapshot icon at the upper-right corner of the graph. This creates an image of the current graph and displays it to the right of the graph, as shown in the following screenshot:

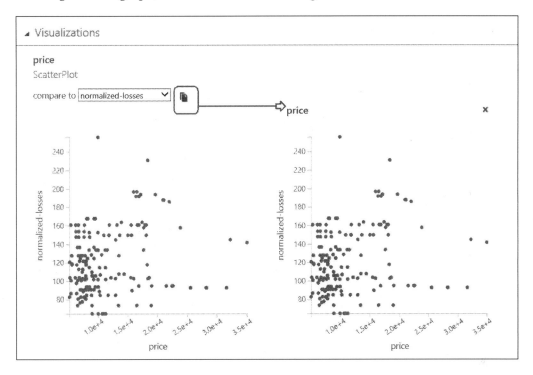

You can create as many snapshots as you want—they will be displayed consecutively to the right of the graph. To close a snapshot, click on the **X** symbol in the upper-right corner of the image.

# Do it yourself

The **Energy Efficiency Regression data** module is another sample dataset available by default in ML Studio under the **Saved Dataset** section. Use the dataset to:

- Visualize the dataset
- Find out the number of rows and columns
- Find out all the numerical and string features
- Find out the basic statistics, such as mean, standard deviation, missing values, and so on
- Plot a histogram for the **Heating Load** feature
- Plot a box plot for the **Cooling Load** feature
- Compare the Heating Load feature with the Cooling Load feature and to observe the scatter plot

# Summary

You have just finished an important chapter. You started with exploring the basic concepts in statistics, such as the mean, standard deviation, and also basic visualization techniques, such as histogram, box and whiskers plot, and scatter plot. You then moved on to explore a dataset by visualizing it in ML Studio. On a visualization pop-up window in ML Studio, you found a report of basic statistics of a dataset. Then, you plotted the features in a graph using a histogram and box plot. You are also capable of comparing two features in a graph.

When you need to work on any data analysis, you need data and you need to import data from different sources. In the next chapter, you will explore different ways you can import data to ML Studio and also ways to export data from ML Studio.

# 4

# Getting Data in and out of ML Studio

For any data analysis, you need data as input. Data analysis generates results as a dataset, which needs to be stored for future use. **ML Studio** allows you to import and export data in a variety of different formats. You can use the `Reader` module to import a dataset in ML Studio from external sources and you can use the `Writer` module to export a dataset. You can also download and upload datasets to and from your PC respectively for different data formats.

ML Studio supports a number of data formats. The internal data format, data table (DotNetTable), is primarily used to move data between modules inside an experiment. When you import data from external sources to ML Studio, the formats supported as of now are ARFF, CSV, Hive Table, SVMLight, Text, and TSV. Let's take a look at the following term list:

- **ARFF**: This is the machine learning data format defined by **Weka**. An **Attribute-Relation File Format** (**ARFF**) file is an ASCII text file that describes a list of instances that share a set of attributes.

- **CSV**: This is a text file where data is contained in a tabular format with different record separated by a line and values (columns) separated by a comma.

- **TSV**: This is a text file similar to CSV where data is contained in a tabular format with different records separated by a line and values (columns) separated by a tab stop character.

- **Hive Table**: This is the data table from **Hadoop** that is accessible via **Hive\***.

- **SVMLight**: This contains the file format training examples of the **SVMLight\*** software.

- **Text**: This is a plain text file.

# Getting data in ML Studio

ML Studio lets you import data from different sources. You can either upload a file from your PC or import data from external sources through the `Data Reader` module.

# Uploading data from a PC

You can follow the given steps to upload a dataset from your PC to ML Studio:

1. Go to ML Studio and create an experiment or go to an existing experiment.
2. Click on the **+NEW** icon at the bottom-left corner of the page, then on **DATASET**, and then on **FROM LOCAL FILE**.
3. The **Upload a new dataset** dialog box is displayed after you click on the icon.
4. Click on **Browse** to select the file that you want to upload.
5. Don't select the tick box for **This is the new version of an existing dataset** unless you are uploading a new version of an existing dataset.
6. Specify a name for the dataset. This will help you identify your dataset when you build your experiment. The dataset name must be unique—you should not have two datasets that have the same name in the saved **Dataset** option. If you are uploading a new version of an existing dataset, then you need to choose the name of the dataset for which you are uploading a new version.
7. Specify the type of data that you are trying to upload.
8. You can optionally provide a description for your data.
9. Then, click on the **OK** button (checkmark) at the bottom-right corner of the popup to start uploading.

During upload, you will see a message that your file is being uploaded. The upload time will depend on the size of your data and the speed of your connection to the service.

After a successful upload, the dataset will appear as a module, like any sample dataset, under **Saved Datasets | My Datasets** in the left-hand side of the module's palette. You can use it inside your experiment and view it by dragging it to the experiment canvas.

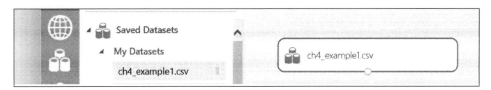

You can also click on the **DATASETS** link on the left-hand side below the **WEB SERVICES** option to find all the uploaded datasets. If you wish to delete any dataset, then select it by clicking on it and click on **DELETE** in the bottom panel of the web page.

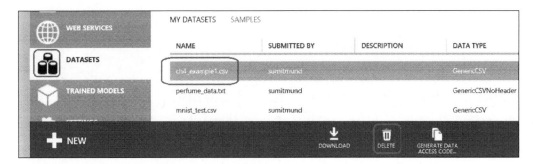

# The Enter Data module

ML Studio comes with the **Enter Data** module, which lets you enter a small set of data manually by typing into it, and lets you construct a dataset quickly and easily. It can be useful to test something quickly.

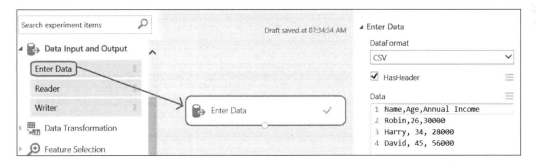

In the preceding example, data is entered using the CSV format and the dataset is marked by ticking the **HasHeader** option, so that it has a header. After running the experiment successfully, you can view the entered dataset by right-clicking on the output port of the module and choosing **Visualize**.

# The Data Reader module

Often, you need to import data from external sources. You can do so using the **Reader** module available under the **Data Input and Output** option. The `Reader` module loads CSV, TSV, and ARFF data files from sources, such as the Web, Azure SQL database, Azure table, Hive Table, or Windows Azure Blob storage. The output port of the module returns the result dataset downloaded from the given data source, which the other connected module can consume.

# Getting data from the Web

You can import a dataset from a web URL in ML Studio through HTTP/HTTPS/FTP/FTPS, although you need to choose the data source for the `Reader` module as HTTP. The following section walks you through the process of how to import a public dataset to ML Studio.

## Fetching a public dataset – do it yourself

The UCI machine learning repository contains different datasets and makes them available for free for anyone who is interested. This URL contains a CSV file that includes the forest fire dataset: `http://archive.ics.uci.edu/ml/machine-learning-databases/forest-fires/forestfires.csv`.

To import the file to ML Studio, follow these steps:

1. Go to ML Studio. Click on the **+NEW** button and choose **EXPERIMENT**.

2. From the modules palette, find the **Reader** module and drag it to the experiment canvas.

3. The module properties pane is displayed on the screen. Choose the data source as **HTTP**.

4. Specify a complete URL: `http://archive.ics.uci.edu/ml/machine-learning-databases/forest-fires/forestfires.csv`.

5. Specify the data format as **CSV**.

6. Indicate that the file contains the column headings by ticking the checkbox **CSV or TSV has header row**. This means that the first row of the file will be considered as a heading row.

7. Run the experiment. After it has been successfully executed, you can find a green tick mark on the module.

8. To view the output data, right-click on the **Reader** module's output port and choose **Visualize**. This opens the results in a new browser window:

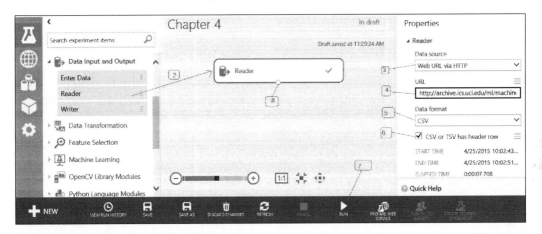

# Getting data from Azure

ML Studio lets you transfer data from the following Azure services:

- **Windows Azure BLOB Storage**: This enables you to read the BLOBs (files) from Windows Azure BLOB storage. If you use the ARFF format for storage, columns are mapped using the header metadata. If you use TSV or CSV formats, mappings are inferred by sampling column data.

- **Windows Azure Table Storage**: This enables you to read data from the flexible NoSQL storage. Built-in and declared data attribute types are mapped directly to metadata (timestamp, integer, and so on).

- **SQL Azure Tables**: This enables you to read selected table data from an SQL Azure database. As this is structured data, metadata mapping is automatic.

# Data format conversion

Sometimes, you may need to convert a dataset to a format that ML Studio supports. There are five data format conversion modules available. All these modules accept a dataset as input, through their input ports and convert the dataset to their respective format. The following are all the modules, and their names are self-explanatory:

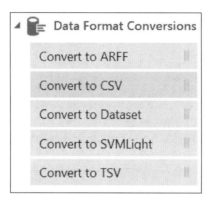

# Getting data from ML Studio

You can also export data from ML Studio to another data destination, you can export it to your PC, or save it to ML Studio itself as a saved dataset item.

# Saving a dataset on a PC

If you want to download a dataset from a module output in ML Studio to your PC, follow the given steps:

1. Right-click on the output port of the module that you want to save as a dataset. Note that you can't download a dataset that is an output in the data table format. In such a case, you have to convert it to the CSV or TSV format to download it. Refer to the following screenshot to see this:

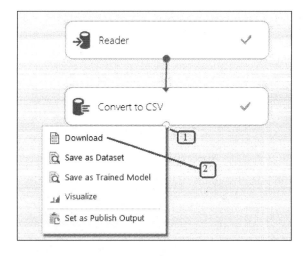

2. Click on **Download** and the file will be downloaded to your PC.

# Saving results in ML Studio

There will be times when you would want to take a result from an experiment and would want to save it in ML Studio for later use. To do this:

1. Right-click on the output port of the module that you want to save as a dataset.

2. Click on the **Save as Dataset** option:

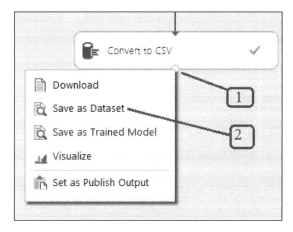

3. When prompted, enter a name that would allow you to identify the dataset easily.

4. Click on the checkbox (this is the new version of an existing dataset) if you want to override an existing one and want to select the name of the existing dataset, otherwise leave it unchecked.

When you have saved, the dataset will be available for use within an experiment and will appear in the dataset list.

## The Writer module

You can use the `Writer` module to write a dataset to Windows Azure BLOB storage, Azure table, Azure SQL Database, or HDFS (which is a Hadoop cluster deployed anywhere, but is accessible) as Hive Query. This module accepts data destination as the first parameter and then other required parameters based on the chosen destination. A `Writer` module that writes a dataset to Azure Blog Storage may look like the following:

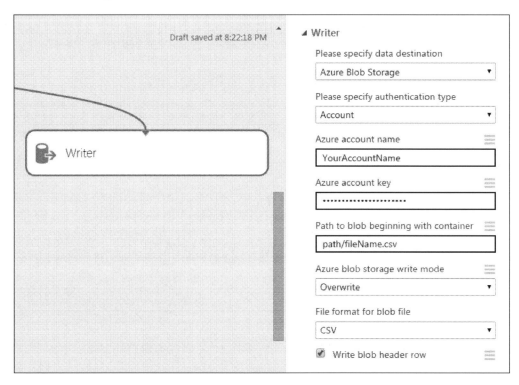

# Summary

We started with exploring the different data formats supported by ML Studio. Then we explored how to import data from external sources and how to export a dataset to external sources. We used the **Reader** module to import and the **Writer** module to export data. You also learned about the **Enter Data** module, which lets you build a small dataset by entering data manually.

After you import data from a source to ML Studio, it often needs some kind of preparation before you apply machine learning algorithms to it. Also, certain machine learning algorithms require certain preprocessing of the data. In the next chapter, we will explore the different data preparation options available with ML Studio.

# 5
# Data Preparation

In practical scenarios, most of the time you would find that the data available for predictive analysis is not fit for the purpose. This is primarily because of two reasons:

- In the real world, data is always messy. It usually has lots of unwanted items, such as missing values, duplicate records, data in different formats, data scattered all around, and so on.

- Quite often, data is either required in a proper format or needs some preprocessing so that it is ready before we apply machine learning algorithms to it for predictive analysis.

So, you need to prepare your data or transform your data to make it fit for the required analysis. ML Studio comes with different options to prepare your data, and in this chapter, you will explore options to preprocess data for some of the common scenarios and ways to prepare data when necessary modules are not readily available with ML Studio. This chapter aims to familiarize you with these options to provide you with an overview of the practical use of most of these options, which you will find in the subsequent chapters.

## Data manipulation

You may need to manipulate data to transform it to the required format. The following are some of the frequently used scenarios and modules available.

## Clean Missing Data

Clean missing data and missing values in data are probably the most common problems you need to fix before data analysis. When missing values are present, certain algorithms may not work or you may not have the desired result. So, you need to get rid of the missing values either by replacing them with some logical values or by removing the existing row(s) or column(s).

ML Studio comes with a module, **Clean Missing Data**, to solve this exact problem. It lets you either remove the rows or columns that have missing values or lets you replace the values in the rows and columns with one of the these: mean, median, mode, custom values, a value that uses the probabilistic form of **Principal Component Analysis (PCA)**, or **Multiple Imputation by Chained Equations (MICE)**. MICE is a statistical technique that updates each column using an appropriate algorithm after initializing the missing entries with a default value. These updates are repeated a number of times and are specified by the `Number of Iterations` parameter. The default option is to replace the values of the rows and columns with a custom value, where you can specify a placeholder value, such as `0` or `NA` that is applied to all missing values. You should be careful that the value you specify matches the data type of the column.

The first output of the module is the cleaned dataset while the second one outputs the transformation that is to be passed to the module to clean new data. You can find the **Clean Missing Data** module under **Data Transformation | Manipulation** in the module palette.

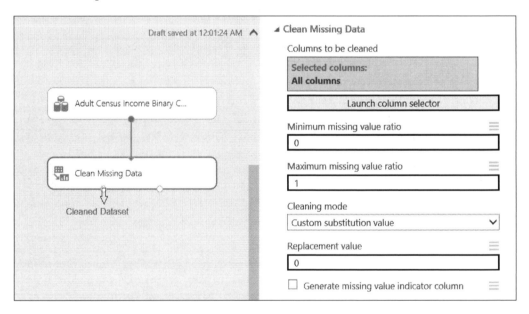

In the last parameter, if you select the check box for **Generate missing value indicator column**, then it will add a new column for each column containing missing values and will indicate the same for each row it finds a missing value for.

# Removing duplicate rows

You use the **Remove Duplicate Rows** module to remove duplicate rows from the input dataset based on the list of columns you specify. Two rows are considered duplicates if the values of all the included columns are equal. This module also takes an input, that is, the **Retain first duplicate row** checkbox, as an indicator that specifies whether to keep the first row of a set of duplicates and discard others or to keep the last duplicate row encountered and discard the rest.

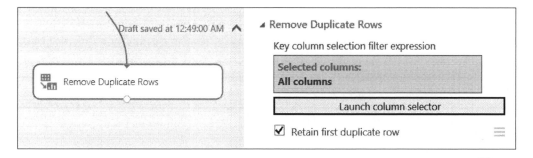

# Project columns

You can use the **Project Columns** module when you have to choose specific columns in a dataset for your analysis. Based on your requirements, you can do this either by excluding all columns and including a few columns. Alternatively, you can start with including all the columns and excluding a few.

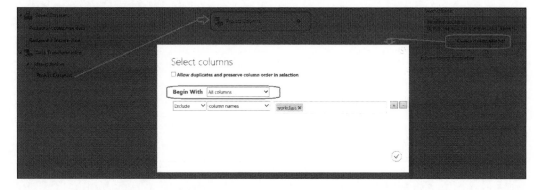

The preceding screenshot illustrates how the **Projects Columns** module just excludes one column from the given dataset. Also notice that you can tick the checkbox on the top, if you like, to keep the duplicate rows' and columns' order in the selection.

# The Metadata Editor module

The **Metadata Editor** module allows you to change the metadata of one or more columns in a dataset. You can change the following for a given dataset:

- You can change the Datatype of columns; for example, string to integer
- You can change the type of columns to categorical or noncategorical; for example, one column may contain user IDs, which are integers, but you may consider them as categorical
- You can change the consideration of column(s) as features or a label; for example, if one dataset has a column that contains income of a population you are interested making a prediction, you may want to consider it as a label or target variable
- You can change the name of a column

Let's take a look at the following screenshot which explains the various functions provided by the **Metadata Editor** module:

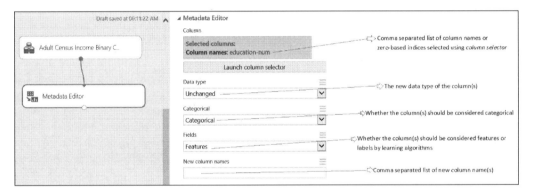

# The Add Columns module

The **Add Columns** module takes two datasets as input and concatenates both by combining all columns from the two datasets to create a single dataset. The resulting dataset will have the sum of the columns of both input datasets.

To add columns of two datasets to a single dataset, you need to keep in mind the following:

- The columns in each dataset must have the same number of rows.

- All the columns from each dataset are concatenated when you use the **Add Columns** option. If you want to add only a subset of the columns, use the **Project Columns** module on the result set to create a dataset with the columns you want.

- If there are two columns with the same name, then a numeric suffix will be added to the column name that comes from the right-hand side input.

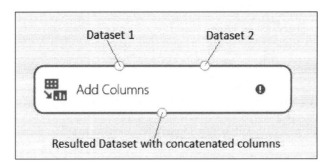

# The Add Rows module

The **Add Rows** module takes two datasets as input and concatenates them by appending the rows of the second dataset after the first dataset.

To add rows of two datasets to a single dataset, you need keep in mind of the following:

- Both the datasets must have the same number of columns

The resulted dataset will have the sum of the number of rows of both the input datasets:

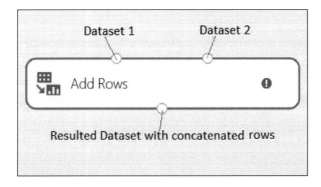

# The Join module

The **Join** module lets you join two datasets. If you are familiar with RDBMS, then you may find it similar to SQL-like join operations; however, no SQL knowledge is required to use it. You can perform the following kinds of join operation:

- **Inner Join**: This is a typical join operation. It returns the combined rows only when the values of the key columns match.

- **Left Outer Join**: This returns the joined rows for all the rows from the left-hand side table. When a row in the left-hand side table has no matching rows in the right-hand side table, the returned row contains the missing values of all the columns coming from the right-hand side table.

- **Full Outer Join**: This returns the joined rows from both datasets with first the result from the **Inner Join** operation and then appends the rows with a mismatch.

- **Left Semi-Join**: This returns just the row from the left-hand side table when the values of the key column(s) match.

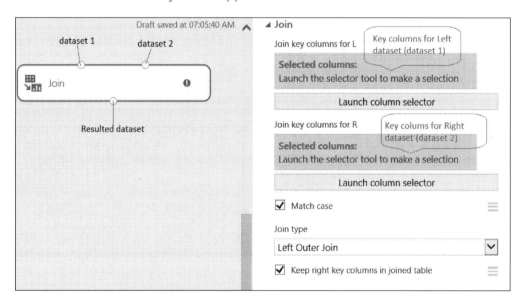

# Splitting data

Quite often, you would need to split your dataset; most commonly, you would need to split a given dataset for analysis into train and test dataset. ML Studio comes with a **Split** module for this purpose. It lets you split your dataset into two datasets based on a specified fraction. So, if you choose **0.8**, it outputs the first dataset with 80 percent of the input dataset, and the rest 20 percent as second output. You also have an option to split the data randomly. You can specify a random seed value other than 0 if you need to get the same result in a random split every time you run it. You can find the **Split** module under **Data Transformation | Sample**, and then Split it in the module palette:

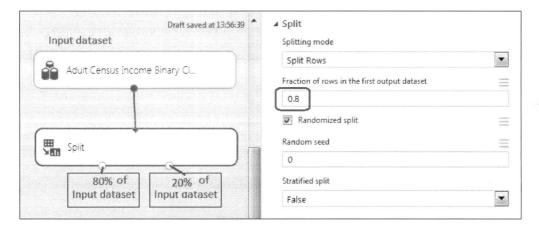

Notice that the last parameter, **Stratified split**, is **False** by default, and you make it **True** only when you go for a stratified split, which means it groups first and then randomly selects rows from each strata (group). In this case, you need to specify the **Stratification key** column based on which grouping will be made.

You can also specify different Splitting modes as the parameter instead of specifying default split rows, such as:

- **The Recommender Split**: You can choose this when you need to split data to use it as train and test data in a recommendation model.

- **The Regular Expression**: You can use this option to specify a regular expression to split the dataset into two sets of rows—rows with values matching the expression and all the remaining rows. The regular expression is applied only to the specified column in the dataset. This splitting option is helpful for a variety of pre-preprocessing and filtering tasks. For example, you can apply a filter on all rows containing the text *Social* by applying the following regular expression to a string column *text Social*.

- **The Relative Expression**: You can use this option and create relational expressions that act as filters on numerical columns; for example, the following expression selects all rows where the values in the column are greater than 2000, such as *ColumnName>2000*.

# Do it yourself

Start a new experiment and drag the sample dataset, the **Adult Census Income Binary Classification** dataset, from the module palette under the **Saved Datasets** group. Then, do the following:

- Visualize the dataset and find out all the columns that have missing values
- Use the **Clean Missing Data** module to replace the missing values with 0
- On the result dataset of the previously used **Metadata Editor** module, select all the columns except income and identify them as feature fields
- On the result dataset of the previously used the **Split** module, split the dataset into 80 percent and 20 percent using the same module
- Run the experiment and visualize the dataset from both the output ports of the **Split** module

Your experiment may look like the following:

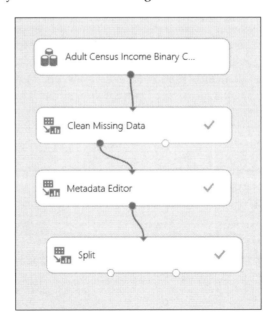

# The Apply SQL Transformation module

The **Apply SQL Transformation** module lets you run a SQL query on the input dataset(s) and get the desired result. You can find it under **Data Transformation | Manipulation** in the module palette. The module can take one, two, or three datasets as inputs. The dataset coming from input 1 can be referenced as **t1**. Similarly, you can refer to datasets from input 2 and input 3 as **t2** and **t3**, respectively. On the properties of the module, the **Apply SQL Transformation** module takes only a parameter as a SQL query. The syntax of the SQL it supports is based on the SQLite standard.

In the following illustration, the module takes data from two datasets, joins them, and selects fewer columns. It also generates calculated columns by applying an aggregation function, AVG.

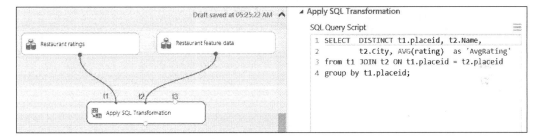

If you are already familiar with SQL, you may find this module very handy for data transformation.

# Advanced data preprocessing

ML Studio also comes with advanced data processing options. The following are some of the common options that are discussed in brief.

# Removing outliers

Outliers are data points that are distinctly separate from the rest of the data. Outliers, if present in your dataset, may cause problems by distorting your predictive model that may result in an unreliable prediction of the data. In many cases, it is a good idea to clip or remove the outliers.

ML Studio comes with the **Clip Values** module, which detects outliers and lets you clip or replace values with a threshold, mean, median, or missing value. By default, it is applied to all the numeric columns, but you can select one or more columns. You can find it by navigating to **Data Transformation | Scale** and then **Reduce** in the module palette.

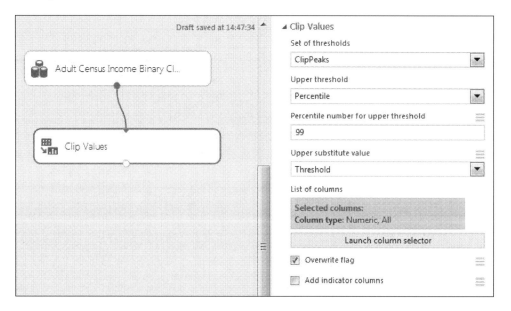

# Data normalization

Often, different columns in a dataset come in different scales; for example, you may have a dataset with two columns: age, with values ranging from 15 to 95, and annual income, with values ranging from $30,000 to $300,000. This may be problematic in some cases where certain machine algorithms require data to be in the same scale.

ML Studio comes with the **Normalize Data** module, which applies a mathematical function to numeric data to make dataset values conform to a common scale; for example, transforming all numeric columns to have values between 0 to 1. By default, the module is applied to all numeric columns, but you can select one or more columns. Also, you can choose from the following mathematical functions:

- Z-Score
- Min-max
- Logistic
- Log-normal
- Tanh

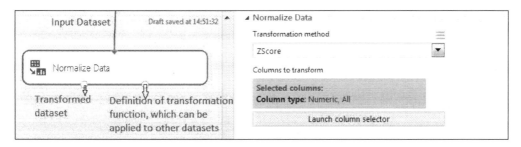

# The Apply Math Operation module

Sometimes, you may need to perform a mathematical operation on your dataset as a part of your data preparation. In ML Studio, you can use the **Apply Math Operation** module, which takes a dataset as input and returns a data table where elements of the selected columns have been transformed by the specified math operation. For unary operations, such as Abs(x), the operation is applied to each of the elements. For binary operations, such as Subtract(x, y), two selections of columns are required and the result is computed over pairs of elements between columns. It gives you a range of mathematical functions grouped under different categories. By default, it is applied to all numeric columns, but you can select one or more columns. You can find it under the **Statistical Functions** module in the module palette.

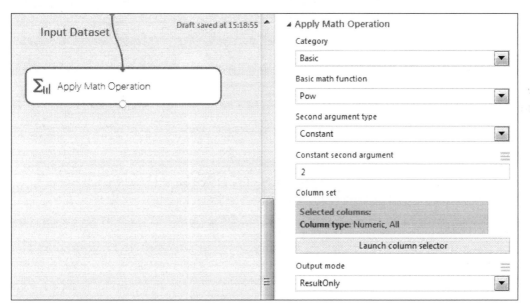

# Feature selection

Not all features or columns in a dataset have the same predictive power. There are times when data contains many redundant or irrelevant features. Redundant features provide no additional information than the currently selected features, and irrelevant features provide no useful information in any context. So, it's ideal to get rid of redundant or irrelevant features from the dataset before applying predictive analysis.

ML Studio comes with the following two modules for feature selection, which takes an input dataset and result dataset with filtered columns or features.

## The Filter Based Feature Selection module

The **Filter Based Feature Selection** module uses different statistical tests to determine a subset of features with the highest predictive power. You can find it under **Feature Selection** in the module palette. It takes a dataset as input that contains two or more feature columns. The first output is a dataset containing the top N predictive-powered features (columns). The second output is a dataset containing the scores assigned to the selected columns (scalars). This module selects the important features from a dataset based on the following heuristic option that you've chosen:

- Pearson's correlation option
- Mutual information option
- Kendall's correlation option
- Spearman's correlation option
- Chi squared option
- Fisher score option
- Count based option

Pearson's correlation is the default option in the **Filter Based Feature Selection** module. It works with numeric, logical, and categorical string columns. You should note that all the heuristics or scoring methods don't work with all types of data. So, your selection of the scoring method depends, in part, on the type of data you have. For more details on these scoring methods, you may refer to the product documentation.

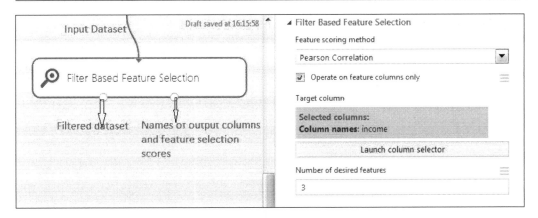

## The Fisher Linear Discriminant Analysis module

The **Fisher Linear Discriminant Analysis** module finds a linear combination of features that characterizes or separates two or more classes of objects or events. The resulting combination is usually used for dimensionality reduction before or after the classification. You can find it under **Feature Selection** in the module palette.

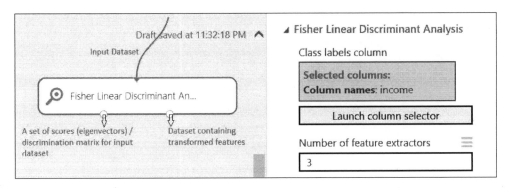

# Data preparation beyond ready-made modules

Though ML Studio comes with many data preprocessing modules, you may come across situations when the available modules don't solve your needs. These are the times you may need to write code in R or Python, run them in ML Studio, and make this part of your experiment. You can find more information on how to write code and extend ML Studio in *Chapter 10, Extensibility with R and Python*.

It is recommended, as of now, that you do any data preparation inside ML Studio if your data size is within a couple of gigabytes (GB). If you are dealing with more data, then you should prepare your data outside ML Studio, say, using an SQL database or using big data technologies, such as Microsoft's cloud-based Hadoop service **HDInsight**. Then, you should consume the prepared data inside ML Studio for predictive analytics.

# Summary

In any data analysis task, data preparation consumes most of your time. In this chapter, you learned about different data preparation options in ML Studio, starting with exploring the importance of data preparation. Then, you familiarized yourself with some of the very common data transformation tasks, such as dealing with missing values, duplicate values, concatenating rows or columns of two datasets, SQL-like joining datasets, selecting columns in a dataset, and splitting a dataset. You also learned how to apply SQL queries to transform datasets. You explored some of the advanced options of transforming a dataset by applying math functions, normalization, and feature selection.

In the next chapter, you can start applying the machine learning algorithm and, in particular, the regression algorithms that come with ML Studio.

# 6
# Regression Models

Finally we are going to start with the machine learning algorithms. You learned earlier that primarily, there are two kinds of supervised machine learning algorithms and regression is one of them. Before you start with different regression algorithms and techniques available with ML Studio, we will try to know more about regression analysis and why it is used.

## Understanding regression algorithms

Consider that you live in a locality and you've got the following dataset that has all the transactions of different properties sold in the area along with the property details. Let's take a look at the following table:

| Property Type | Area (Sq feet) | Price ($) |
|---|---|---|
| D | 2000 | 500,000 |
| T | 1500 | 200,000 |
| F | 1400 | 300,000 |
| T | 1000 | 100,000 |
| F | 2000 | 450,000 |
| S | 1800 | 350,000 |
| D | 2500 | 700,000 |
| F | 1500 | 350,000 |

Here, **D** means detached, **S** means semi detached, **T** means terraced, and **F** means flats/maisonettes.

Now, a flat is going to be available on the market of the size; 1,800 square feet. You need to predict the price at which it will be sold. This is a regression problem because you need to predict a number for the target variable. Here, the property price is the target variable and the **Property Type** and **Area** are the two features or dependent variables. A target variable in machine learning is also known as a label.

You need to come up with a model that will take the value for the Property Type and Area and output the price. Consider the model as a mathematical function *f(Property Type, Area) = Predicted Price.*

The actual price at which the property will be sold may or may not be the same as the predicted price. The difference between the actual price and the predicted price is the error. While building a prediction model, you should try to minimize the error so that the predicted value can be as close to the actual value as possible.

Extending the preceding example, you have supposedly built a model and predicted the value for a 1800 square feet flat using the following formula:

f(F, 1800) = $400,000

So, $400,000 is the predicted value, and consider that $410,000 is the actual value at which the property was sold. Then, the error would be *Error = $410,000 - $400,000 = $10,000.*

# Train, score, and evaluate

Before making the prediction, you need to train an algorithm with the example data or training dataset where the target value or the label is known. After training the model, you can make a prediction with the trained model.

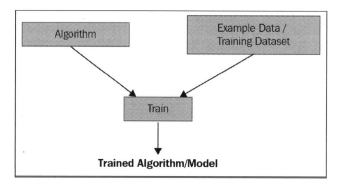

Continuing with the preceding illustration, the trained model may be considered as the mathematical function f to make a prediction.

Usually, when you have to build a model from a given dataset, you split the dataset into two sets and use one as a training dataset and the other as a test dataset. After the model is trained with the training data, you use the test dataset to see how the model is performing, that is, how many errors it has.

After the model is trained, you can use the test data to make a prediction or to score. In scoring, the feature values are used and then the target value is predicted. At this point, you are not sure how your model is performing. You need to evaluate it to find out its performance. During evaluation, you take the scored value and the actual value, which is known as you have split your dataset into train and test.

Continuing with the previous illustration, while scoring, you find out that the predicted price of a 1800 square feet flat will be $400,000 and during evaluation, you discover that there is an error of $10,000.

Overall, during experimentation you can follow the given steps:

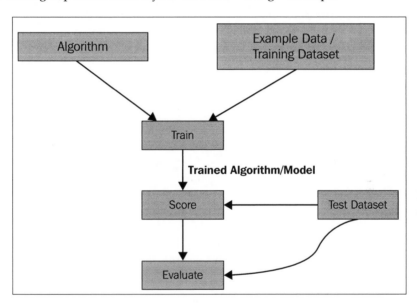

ML Studio provides different statistics to measure error and performance of your regression model. It also comes with a set of algorithms to experiment with your dataset.

# The test and train dataset

Usually, you train an algorithm with your **Train** dataset and validate or test your model with a test dataset. In practice, most of the time, you are given one dataset. So, you may need to split the given dataset into two and use one as a train and the other as test. Usually, the training set consists of bigger parts and the test set consists of smaller parts, say 70-30 or 80-20. Ideally, while splitting the original dataset, it is split randomly. The **Split** module in ML Studio solves the purpose well.

# Evaluating

Consider the previous illustration of the dataset (refer to table 6.1) as a train dataset and the following as a test dataset:

| Property type | Area (Sq feet) | Actual Price ($) | Predicted price ($) |
|---|---|---|---|
| F | 1800 | 400,000 | 410,000 |
| T | 1700 | 220,000 | 210,000 |

Consider the actual price and predicted/scored price for the first row as *y1* and *f1*, respectively. So, in the preceding table, we can make out that *y1 = 400,000* and *f1 = 410,000*.

Similarly, we can make out for the second row that *y2 = 220,000* and *f2 = 210,000*.

ML Studio provides the following statistics to measure how a model is performing.

# The mean absolute error

**The mean absolute error** (**MAE**) is a quantity used to measure how close forecasts or predictions are to the eventual outcomes. It is calculated as the average of the absolute difference between the actual values and the predicted values. Let's take a look at the following figure:

$$ \text{MAE} = \frac{1}{n} \sum_{i=1}^{n} \left| f_i - y_i \right| $$

Here $f_i$ is the prediction and $y_i$ is the true value.

It has the same unit as the original data and it can only be compared between models whose errors are measured in the same units.

# The root mean squared error

**The root mean squared error** (**RMSE**) is calculated by taking the square root of the average of the square of all the errors (which is the difference between the predicted and actual value). Let's take a look at the following figure:

$$RMSE = \sqrt{\frac{\sum\limits_{i=1}^{n}(f_i - y_i)^2}{n}}$$

Here, $f_i$ is the prediction and $y_i$ is the true value

It can only be compared between models whose errors are measured in the same units.

# The relative absolute error

**The relative absolute error** (**RAE**) is the average of the absolute error relative to the average of the absolute difference of the mean of the actual value and actual values. Let's take a look at the following figure:

$$RAE = \frac{\sum\limits_{i=1}^{n}|f_i - y_i|}{\sum\limits_{i=1}^{n}|\overline{y} - y_i|}$$

Here $f_i$ is the prediction, $y_i$ is the actual or the true value and $\overline{y}$ is the mean of $y_i$.

It can be compared between models whose errors are measured in different units.

# The relative squared error

**The relative squared error** (**RSE**) is the average of the squared difference of the predicted value and the actual value relative to the average of the squared difference, average of the actual value and actual values.

$$RSE = \frac{\sum_{i=1}^{n}(f_i - y_i)^2}{\sum_{i=1}^{n}(\bar{y} - y_i)^2}$$

Here $f_i$ is the prediction, $y_i$ is the true value, and $\bar{y}$ is the mean of $y_i$.

It can be compared between models whose errors are measured in different units.

## The coefficient of determination

The coefficient of determination $R2$ summarizes the explanatory power of the regression model. If the regression model is perfect, though not practical, $R2$ is 1.

$$Coefficient\ of\ Determination, R^2 = \frac{SSR}{SST}$$

$$Sum\ of\ Squares\ Regression,\ SSR = \sum_{i}^{n}(f_i - \bar{y})^2$$

$$Sum\ of\ Squares\ Total,\ SST = \sum_{i}^{n}(y_i - \bar{y})^2$$

Here $f_i$ is the prediction, $y_i$ is the true value, and $\bar{y}$ is the mean of $y_i$

The coefficient of determination can also be interpreted as the percent of the data that fits in the model. For example, if $R2 = 0.7950$, then 79 percent of the total variation in $y$ can be explained by the linear relationship between features and $y$, the response variable (or the target variable).

So, for your model, the closer $R2$ is to 1, the better it is. For all other the error statistics, the less the value, the better it is.

# Linear regression

**Linear regression** is one of the regression algorithms available in ML Studio. It tries to fit a line to the dataset. It is a popular algorithm and probably the oldest regression algorithm. We will use it to train the model to make prediction for one of the sample datasets available: automobile price data (Raw). This dataset is about automobiles distinguished by their make and model and other features. It also includes price. More information on the dataset can be found at `https://archive.ics.uci.edu/ml/datasets/Automobile`.

We will use price as a label or the target variable here. So, given the automobile features, you need to predict the price of the automobile.

Go to ML Studio and create a new experiment. Then, expand **Saved Datasets** in the modules palette to the left of the screen. Drag the **Automobile price data (Raw)** module to the canvas.

Then, expand **Data Transformation** and then **Sample and Split** in the modules palette and drag the **Split** module to the canvas. Set the **Fraction of rows** parameter in the first output dataset to **0.8** and leave the others to their default values. You are splitting the dataset so that 80 percent of the data will be used to train and the other 20 percent will be used for test.

After you are ready with your train and test data, drag the **Train** module to canvas. Type `train` in the search box in the modules palette to the left of the screen and when the **Train** module appears, drag it to the canvas. Then, join the first output of the **Split** module to the second input of the **Train** module. Now, you need to select the column of the dataset that will be your target variable, or for which you will train a model to make a prediction. In our case, *price* is the target variable or label for which you are going to make a prediction.

Select the **Train** module by clicking on it, expand the properties pane to the right of the screen, and click on the **Launch column selector** option.

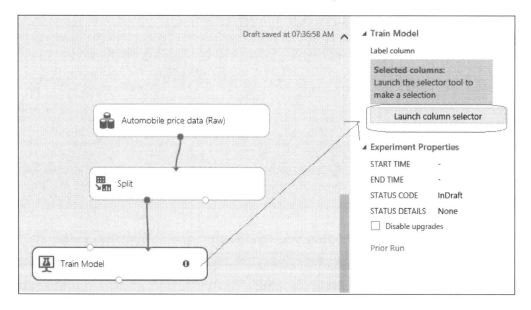

Then, the pop up to select a column will appear. Type price in the textbox to the right of the screen and click on the tickbox to select the column.

Likewise, drag the **Linear Regression** module to the canvas. Type linear in the search box in the modules palette to the left of the screen and when the module appears, drag it to the canvas.

Then, select the **Linear Regression** module and leave the property values at default. Use **0** for the **Random number seed** option. The **Random number seed** option is used to generate a random number that is used for reproducible results.

Now, join the output of the **Linear Regression** module to the first input port of the **Train** module. It should look like something similar to the following screenshot:

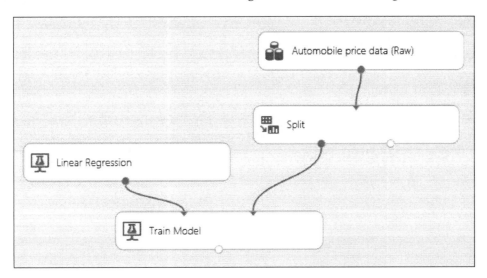

Next, drag the **Score Model** and the **Evaluate Model** modules to the canvas.

The **Score Model** will generate the predicted price value for the test dataset using the trained algorithm. So, it takes two inputs: first, the trained model and second, the test dataset. It generates the scored dataset that contains the predicted values. The **Evaluate Model** takes a scored dataset and generates an evaluation matrix. It can also take two scored datasets so that you can compare two models side by side.

Connect the output of the **Train Model** to the first input of the **Score Model** and the second output of the **Split** module to the second input. Then, connect the output of the **Score Model** to the first input of the **Evaluate Model**.

The complete model may look as follows. Now, click on the **Run** button to run the experiment.

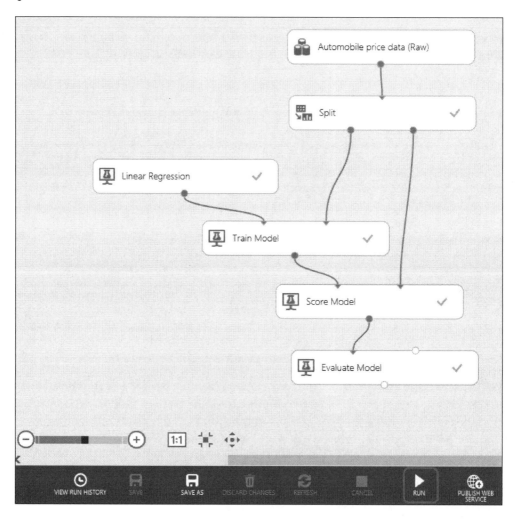

After the run is complete and you see the green tick mark on all the module boxes, you can see the evaluation matrix to find out how your model is performing. To do so, right-click on the output of the **Evaluate Model** and select the **Visualize** option by clicking on it.

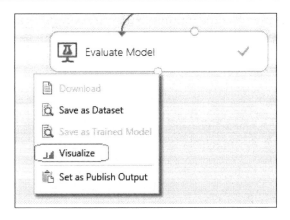

The following popup displays the **Evaluation Results** graph, as shown in the following screenshot:

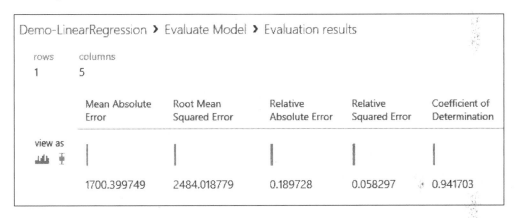

Demo-LinearRegression ❯ Evaluate Model ❯ Evaluation results

rows: 1
columns: 5

| | Mean Absolute Error | Root Mean Squared Error | Relative Absolute Error | Relative Squared Error | Coefficient of Determination |
|---|---|---|---|---|---|
| view as | 1700.399749 | 2484.018779 | 0.189728 | 0.058297 | 0.941703 |

As you can see, **Coefficient of Determination** is **0.941703**, which is decent and the model seems to be performing well.

If you had noticed, you have trained this linear regression model using the Ordinary Least Squared method. You could also have used the Online Gradient Descent with proper parameters, such as the learning rate and number of epochs (iterations). While working with a large dataset, this method can be quite useful as it scales very well. However, working with a few thousand data points in a dataset's Ordinary Least Squared method might be the choice for you as it is simple and easy to train (with a few parameters to choose from).

To keep it simple, in the preceding and following illustrations in this chapter, we have started modeling without initial data preparation, such as removing missing values or choosing the right set of columns or features. In practice, you should always do initial data preparation before training with a dataset. Again, some algorithms require data to be in the proper format to generate the desired result.

# Optimizing parameters for a learner – the sweep parameters module

To successfully train a model, you need to come up with the right set of property values for an algorithm. Most of the time, doing this is not an easy task. First, you need to have a clear understanding of the algorithm and the mathematics behind it. Second, you have to run an experiment many times, trying out many combinations of parameters for an algorithm. At times, this can be very time consuming and daunting.

For example, in the same preceding example, what should be the right value for L2 regularization weight? It is used to reduce overfitting of the model. A model overfits when it performs well on a training dataset, but performs badly on any new dataset. By reducing overfitting, you generalize the model. However, the problem here is that you have to manually adjust this L2 regularization weight, which can be done by trying different values, running the experiment many times, and evaluating its performance in each run.

ML Studio comes with a sweet solution to this in the form of the **Sweep Parameters** module. Instead of a **Train Model** module, you can use the **Train Model** module to generate a trained model optimized with the right set of parameters or property values. The following screenshot describes its inputs and outputs:

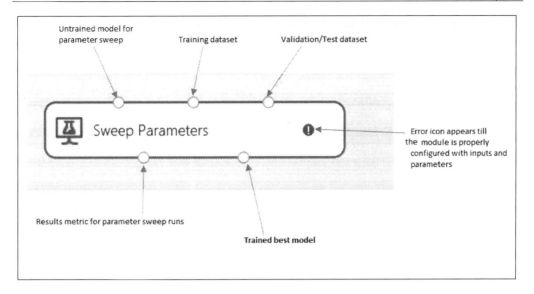

You need to specify a parameter sweeping mode as a parameter of this module. You have two options to specify the parameter of sweeping mode, they are as follows:

- **Entire grid**: This option is useful for cases where you don't know what the best parameter settings might be and want to try many parameters. It loops over a grid predefined by the system to try different combinations and identify the best learner.

- **Random Sweep**: Alternatively, you can choose this option and specify the maximum number of runs that you want the module to execute. It will randomly select parameter values over a range of a limited number of sample runs. This option is suggested when you want to increase the model's performance using the metrics of your choice and conserve computing resources.

You also need to choose a target or label column along with specifying a value for metric to measure the performance of regression, which can be one of the five evaluation matrices, for example, the root mean squared error. While working on a regression problem, you may ignore the parameter setting for classification.

# The decision forest regression

Decision forest, or random forest as it is widely known, is a very popular algorithm. Internally, it constructs many decision trees and then ensembles them as a forest. Each decision tree generates a prediction and in the forest, the predicted values of each tree is averaged out. It works well even in the case of noisy data.

However, to train a decision forest, you need to set the right parameters, for example, the number of decision trees. We will now train a decision forest and optimize its parameters with the **Sweep Parameters** module.

As in the previous case, create a new experiment and give a name to it. Then, do the same steps and expand **Saved Datasets** in the modules palette to the left of the screen. Drag the **Automobile price data (Raw)** module to the canvas.

Then, expand **Data Transformation** and **Sample and Split** in the modules palette and drag the **Split** module to the canvas. Set the **Fraction** parameter of the rows in the first output dataset to **0.8** and leave the others to their default values. You are splitting the dataset so that 80 percent of the data will be used for train and the other 20 percent will be used as test.

Type sweep in the search box in the modules palette to the left of the screen and when the **Sweep Parameters** module appears, drag it to the canvas. Then, join the first output of the **Split** module to the second input of the **Sweep Parameters** module and join the second output of the **Split** module to the third input of the **Sweep Parameters** module.

Now, you need to set the column of the dataset that is your target or label column for which you will train a model to do a prediction. In our case, **price** is the target variable or label for which you are going to make a prediction. Also, set the sweeping mode to **Entire grid** and **Metric for measuring performance for regression** to **Coefficient of determination**.

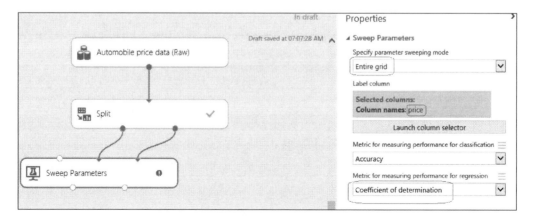

Likewise, drag the **Decision Forest Regression** module to the canvas. Type
Decision Forest in the search box in the modules palette to the left of the screen
and when the module appears, drag it to the canvas. Set the **Resampling method**
property to **Bagging** and leave the rest with their default values, as you can see in the
following screenshot:

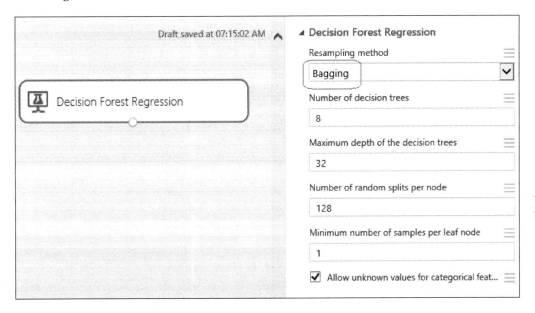

Then, connect the only output of the **Decision Forest Regression** module to the first
input of the **Sweep Parameters** module.

Next, drag the **Score Model** and **Evaluate Model** to the canvas. Connect the second output of the **Sweep Parameters** module to the first input of the **Score Model** and connect the second output of the **Split** module to the second input of the **Score Model**. Then, connect the output of the **Score Model** to the first input of the **Evaluate Model**.

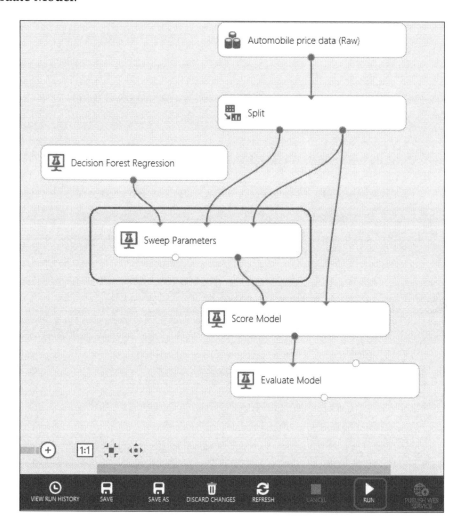

Now, run the experiment and after completion, visualize the output of the **Evaluate Model** to know the performance of the model.

If you are interested to know about the optimum parameters for the **Decision Forest Regression** module obtained by the **Sweep Parameters** module, then right-click on the **Sweep Parameter** module's output port and click on **Visualize**. In the preceding case, it looked as follows:

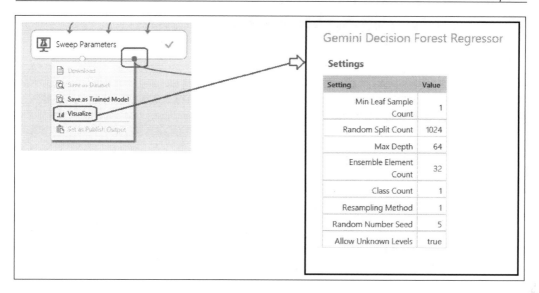

# The train neural network regression – do it yourself

Neural network is a kind of machine learning algorithm inspired by the computational models of a human brain. For regression, ML Studio comes with the Neural Network Regression module. You can train this using the Sweep Parameters module. First, try to train it without the Sweep Parameters module (with the Train module) with default parameters for Neural Network Regression and then train it with the Sweep Parameters module. Note the improvement in performance of the model.

# Comparing models with the evaluate model

With the **Evaluate Model**, you can also compare two models side by side in the same experiment. The two input ports of the module can take the output from the two Score modules and generate the evaluation matrix to compare the output from the two inputs that the module accepts. As shown in the following screenshot:

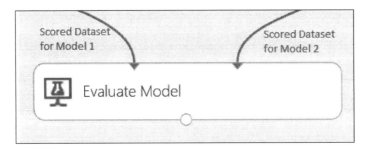

# Comparing models – the neural network and boosted decision tree

The **Boosted Decision Tree Regression** module is another regression algorithm that comes with ML Studio. It is an ensemble model like decision forest, but is a bit different.

Here, we will use both the **Boosted Decision Tree Regression** and **Neural Network Regression** modules in the same experiment and compare both using the **Evaluate Model**. We will use the **Sweep Parameters** module in both cases, to train the algorithm.

Create a new experiment and drag the same sample dataset—the **Automobile price data (Raw)** module. Then, use the two algorithms with the same training dataset (80 percent) and also score using the other 20 percent. The constructed model may look like the following:

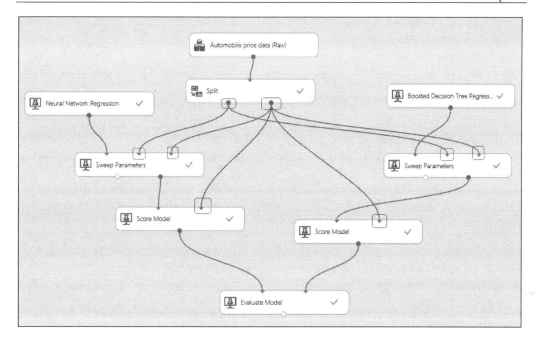

While the connections are straight-forward and intuitive, the connection for the **Sweep Parameters** module for both the cases might be confusing. Note that the inputs with the red circles are coming from the same output of the **Split** module also marked with a red circle. So, the two **Sweep Parameters** modules accept the same training data, but different algorithms to train with. Also, note the input ports marked with the blue circle coming from the same output port of the **Split** module also marked with a blue circle.

After you run the experiment successfully, all the boxes will have a green tick mark. Then, right-click on the output port of the **Evaluate Model** to find the comparison metrics for both the algorithms. Let's take a look at the following screenshot:

| Mean Absolute Error | Root Mean Squared Error | Relative Absolute Error | Relative Squared Error | Coefficient of Determination |
|---|---|---|---|---|
| 5071.800876 | 7664.589306 | 0.565904 | 0.555025 | 0.444975 |
| 1340.164661 | 1958.367584 | 0.149534 | 0.036235 | 0.963765 |

The first row in the preceding screenshot shows the metrics for the model connected to the first input of the **Evaluate Model** and in this case, it shows the **Neural Network Regression** module and the second row for the second model: the **Boosted Decision Tree Regression** module. You know that for better performing models, error values should be as less as possible and the coefficient of determination should be as close as possible to 1, which means that the higher it is the better. As you will find, the Boosted Decision Tree outperforms the Neural Network for this dataset on every evaluation statistic, for example, the **Coefficient of Determination** is **0.963765** versus **0.444975**. Similarly, the relative absolute error is much less for the Boosted Decision Tree as compared to others. If you have to choose between these two models, then in this case, you will naturally choose the Boosted Decision Tree. Because we have not set a random number seed, your results (figures) may be slightly different; however, overall, it doesn't make any difference.

Here, you compared only two models. In practice, you can and should compare as many models as possible on the same problem to find out the best performing model among them.

# Other regression algorithms

Azure ML comes with a bunch of popular regression algorithms. This section briefly describes other algorithms available (at the time of writing of this book) that we have not discussed so far:

- **The Bayesian Linear Regression Model**: This model uses Bayesian Inference for regression. This may not be difficult to train as long as you get the regularization parameter right, which may fit a value such as 0.1, 0.2, and so on.

- **The Ordinal Regression Model**: You use this when you have to train a model for a dataset in which the labels or target values have a natural ordering or ranking among them.

- **The Poisson Regression**: It is a special type of regression analysis. It is typically used for model counts, for example, modeling the number of cold and flu cases associated with airplane flights or estimating the number of calls related to an event or promotion and so on.

# No free lunch

The *No Free Lunch* theorem is related to machine learning and it popularly states the limitation of any machine learning model. As per the theorem, there is no model that fits the best for every problem. So, one model that fits well for one problem in a domain may not hold good for another. So in practice ,whenever you are solving a problem, you need to try out different models and experiment with your dataset to choose the best one. This is especially true for supervised learning; you use the **Evaluate Model** module in ML Studio to assess the predictive accuracies of multiple models of varying complexity to find the best model. A model that works well could also be trained by multiple algorithms, for example, linear regression in ML Studio can be trained by Ordinary Least Square or Online Gradient Descent.

# Summary

You started the chapter by understanding predictive analysis with regression and explored the concepts of training, testing, and evaluating a regression model. You then proceeded to carry on building experiments with different regression models, such as linear regression, decision forest, neural network, and boosted decision trees inside ML Studio. You learned how to score and evaluate a model after training. You also learned how to optimize different parameters for a learning algorithm with the Sweep Parameters module. The No Free Lunch theorem teaches us not to rely on any particular algorithm for every kind of problem, so in ML Studio you should train and evaluate the performance of different models before finalizing a single one.

In the next chapter, you will explore another kind of unsupervised learning called classification and you will explore the different algorithms available with ML Studio.

# 7
# Classification Models

Classification is another kind of supervised machine learning. In this chapter, before getting into the details of building a classification model using ML Studio, you will start with gaining the basic knowledge about a classification algorithm and how a model is evaluated. Then, you will build models with different datasets using different algorithms.

## Understanding classification

Consider you are given the following hypothetical dataset containing data of patients: the size of the tumor in their body, their age, and a class that justifies whether they are affected by cancer or not, 1 being positive (affected by cancer) and 0 being negative (not affected by cancer):

| Age | Tumor size | Class |
|-----|-----------|-------|
| 22  | 135       | 0     |
| 37  | 121       | 0     |
| 18  | 156       | 1     |
| 55  | 162       | 1     |
| 67  | 107       | 0     |
| 73  | 157       | 1     |
| 36  | 123       | 0     |
| 42  | 189       | 1     |
| 29  | 148       | 0     |

Here, the patients are classified as cancer-affected or not. A new patient comes in at the age 17 and is diagnosed of having a tumor the of size 149. Now, you need to predict the classification of this new patient based on the previous data. That's classification for you as you need to predict the class of the dependent variable; here it is **0** or **1**—you may also think of it as true or false.

For a regression problem, you predict a number, for example, the housing price or a numerical value. In a classification problem, you predict a categorical value, though it may be represented with a number, such as **0** or **1**.

You should not be confused between a regression and classification problem. Consider a case where you need to predict the housing price not as a number, but as categories, such as greater than 100K or less than 100K. In this case, though you are predicting the housing price, you are indeed predicting a class or category for the housing price and hence, it's a classification problem.

You build a classification model by training an algorithm with the given training data. In the training dataset, the class or target variable is already known.

# Evaluation metrics

Suppose that you have built a model and trained a classification algorithm with the dataset in Table 7.1 as the training data. Now, you are using the following table as your test data. As you can see, the last column has the predicted class.

| Age | Tumor size | Actual class | Predicted class | |
|-----|-----------|--------------|-----------------|-----|
| 32 | 135 | 0 | 0 | TN |
| 47 | 121 | 0 | 1 | FP |
| 28 | 156 | 1 | 0 | FN |
| 45 | 162 | 1 | 1 | TP |
| 77 | 107 | 0 | 1 | FP |

# True positive

This is the number of times an actual class was positive and was predicted as positive. For example, the patient is actually affected by cancer and the model is also predicted positive.

In our preceding example, there is one instance where the **Actual Class = 1** and **Predicted Class = 1**. So here, **TP = 1**.

# False positive

This is the number of times an actual class was negative and was predicted as positive. For example, the patient is actually *not* affected by cancer but the model is predicted as positive.

In our preceding example, there are two instances where the **Actual Class = 0** and **Predicted Class = 1**. So here, **FP = 2**.

# True negative

This is the number of times an actual class was negative and it was predicted as negative. For example, the patient is actually NOT affected by cancer and the model also predicted it as negative.

In our preceding example, there was one instance where the **Actual Class** = 0 and **Predicted Class** = 0. So here, **TN = 1**.

# False negative

This is the number of times an actual class was positive but was predicted as negative. For example, the patient is actually affected by cancer but the model predicted it as negative.

In our preceding example, there was one instance where the **Actual Class** = 1 and **Predicted Class** = 0. So here, **FN = 1**.

The following table shows **TP**, **TN**, **FP**, and **FN** in a matrix:

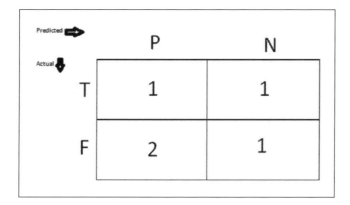

# Accuracy

It is the proportion of a true prediction to the total number of predictions. While true prediction is $TP + TN$, the total number of predictions are of the size of a test dataset, which is also $TP + TN + FP + FN$. So, accuracy can be represented in a formula as follows:

Accuracy = (TP + TN) / (TP + TN + FP + FN)

So in our example, *Accuracy = (1 + 1) / (1 + 1 + 2 + 1) = 2/5 = .4*.

Accuracy can also be represented as a percentage of the prediction that was accurate. So, in our example, accuracy is 40 percent.

Note that the preceding figures are just for illustration of how the calculation is done. In practice, when you build a model, it should have an accuracy of more than 50 percent; otherwise, the model is no good because even a random trial will have 50 percent accuracy.

# Precision

The positive predictive value or precision is the proportion of positive cases that the model has correctly identified. Precision can be represented in the formula form, as follows:

$$\text{Precision} = TP / (TP + FP)$$

So in our example, *Precision = 1 / ( 1+1) = 1/2 = .5.*

# Recall

Sensitivity or recall is the proportion of actual positive cases that are correctly identified. The formula for recall is:

*Recall = TP / (TP + FN)*

So in our example, *Recall = 1 / (1 +2) = 1/3 = .33.*

# The F1 score

The F1 Score can be defined as a formula, as follows:

*F1 = 2TP / (2TP + FP + FN)*

The F1 Score can also be defined in terms of precision (P) and recall (R), as follows:

*F1 = 2PR/(P+R)*

So in our example, *F1 = (1 \* 2) / {(1 \* 2) + 2 + 1 } = 2/ (2 + 2 +1) = 2/5 =.4.*

# Threshold

Threshold is the value above which the threshold belongs to the first class and all the other values belong to the second class. For example, if the threshold is **0.5**, then any patient who has scored more than or equal to **0.5** is identified as sick; otherwise, the patient is identified as healthy. You can think of threshold as probability. To illustrate, if there is a probability of 80 percent or **.8** percent that it may rain today, then you may predict that rain for today is true. Similarly, if it is less than **.8**, then you can predict that it won't rain. So your prediction would depend on the threshold here.

# Understanding ROC and AUC

The **receiver operating characteristics** (**ROC**) graph is a two-dimensional graph in which the true positive rate (TP) is plotted on the $y$ axis and the false positive rate (FP) is plotted on the x axis. An ROC graph depicts the relative tradeoffs between benefits (true positives) and costs (false positives).

The **Area Under the Curve** (**AUC**) is a portion of the area under the ROC curve of the unit square; its value will always be between *0* and *1*, where *1* is the best case or everything is predicted correctly. However, because random guessing produces the diagonal line between *(0, 0)* and *(1, 1)*, which has an area of **0.5**, no realistic classifier should have an AUC less than **0.5**. AUC is often used as a measure of quality of a classification model.

In the following diagram, the blue curve shows the ROC while the area painted in red shows the AUC. The yellow painted diagonal line represents the random guessing:

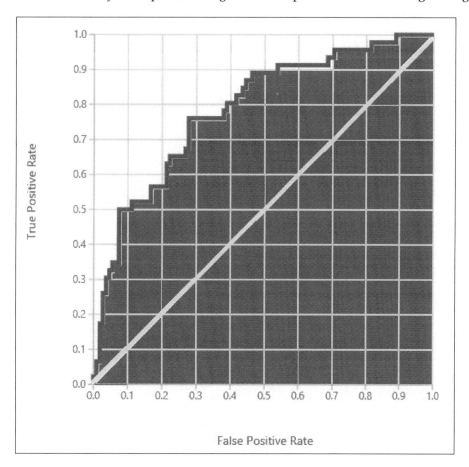

# Motivation for the matrix to consider

While choosing an algorithm for your model, you will have to rely on the preceding metrics that are defined. Often, one metric may not be sufficient to take a decision. To start with, you may look at accuracy, but at times it might be deceptive. Consider a case where you are making a prediction for a rare disease where in reality, 99 percent negative cases and 1 percent of positive cases appear. If your classification model predicts all the cases as true negatives, then the accuracy is still 99 percent. In this case, the F1 score might be useful as it would give you a clear picture. AUC might also be useful for this.

Consider another scenario. Let's stick to our disease prediction example. Suppose you are predicting whether a patient has cancer or not. If you predict a false case (where the patient is NOT affected by the disease) as true, it's a false positive case. In the practical scenario, after such a prediction, the patient will have further medical tests to manually declare as not affected by cancer. However, if you have a predicted true case (where the patient is actually affected by the disease) as false, then it's a false negative case. In practical scenarios, after such a prediction, the patient is left free and allowed to go home without medication. This might be dangerous as the patient might lose life. You may never like to make such a prediction. In such a scenario, as in this story, you may reduce the threshold value to reduce the chance of releasing any true positive cases. Hence, it would result in higher recall and lower precision.

In the scenario opposite to the preceding, say you have a classification model to predict the fraud for an online transaction. Here, predicting a case as fraud, (which is actually not—a case of false positive) may result in poor customer satisfaction. So in this scenario, you may increase the threshold value and hence it would result in higher precision and lower recall.

As you may find from the preceding definition, the F1 score is a balanced approach for measurement, which involves both precision and recall.

When you are not too worried about precision and recall or you are not so sure about them, you can just follow the value of AUC (the higher the better). Many find AUC the best way to measure the performance of a classification model. AUC also provides a graphical representation. However, it is always a good idea to take a note of more than one metric.

# Training, scoring, and evaluating modules

As with regression problems, which you saw in the previous chapter, with classification problems, you can start with an algorithm and train it with data. You can then score ideally with the test data and evaluate the performance of the model.

Navigate to the **Train | Score | Evaluate** option on the screen.

The **Train**, **Score**, and **Evaluate** modules are the same as you used for regression. The **Train** module requires the name of the target (class) variable. The **Evaluate** module generates evaluation metrics for classification.

If you want to tune parameters of an algorithm by parameter sweeping, you can use the same **Sweep Parameters** module.

# Classifying diabetes or not

The **Pima Indians Diabetes Binary Classification dataset** module is present as a sample dataset in ML Studio. It contains all of the data of female patients of the same age belonging to Pima Indian heritage. The data includes medical data, such as glucose and insulin levels, as well as lifestyle factors of the patients. The columns in the dataset are as follows:

- Number of times pregnant
- Plasma glucose concentration of 2 hours in an oral glucose tolerance test
- Diastolic blood pressure (mm Hg)
- Triceps skin fold thickness (mm)
- 2-hour serum insulin (mu U/ml)
- Body mass index (weight in kg/(height in m)^2)
- Diabetes pedigree function
- Age (years)
- Class variable (0 or 1)

The last column is the target variable or class variable that takes the value 0 or 1, where 1 is positive or affected by diabetes and 0 means that the patient is not affected.

You have to build models that could predict whether a patient has diabetes or tests positive or not.

# Two-class bayes point machine

Two-class Bayes Point Machine is a simple-to-train yet powerful linear classifier. We will build our first classification model using it.

Start a new experiment. On the left-hand side module palette on the screen, expand the **Saved Datasets** option, scroll down, and drag the **Pima Indians Diabetes Binary Classification dataset** module to the canvas. Alternatively, you could just type `pima` in the search box to locate the module and then drag it.

Right-click on its output port and click on the **Visualize** option to explore the dataset. You can note that it now has 768 rows and 9 columns.

You have to split this dataset into two to prepare your train and test dataset. So, drag the **Split** module to the canvas and connect the output of the dataset module to the input of the **Split** module. Set **0.8** as the parameter; the **Fraction of rows** option is the first output dataset that splits itself in the ratio of 80:20 to get your train and test dataset, respectively.

Drag the **Two-Class Bayes Point Machine** module, which you can find by navigating to **Machine Learning | Initialize Model | Classification** on the left-hand side module's palette to the canvas.

This module has three parameter values to set. The **Number of training iterations** module is the value that decides the number of times the algorithm iterates over the dataset. The default value **30** is sufficient most of the time. The **Include bias** checkbox if ticked or set to true, adds a constant feature or bias to each instance in training and prediction. The default value is true and it is required to be true most of the time. The last parameter, **Allow unknown values in categorical features**, if ticked or set to true, creates an additional level for each categorical column. Any levels in the test dataset not available in the training dataset are mapped to this additional level. Unless you are doing the required data preprocessing, it is suggested that you tick this or leave it at the default value.

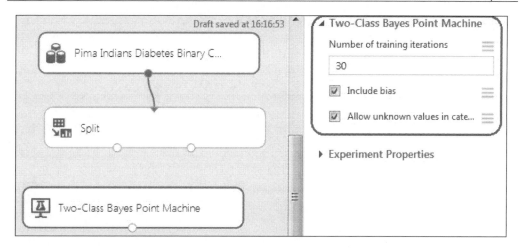

Drag the **Train Model** module to the canvas and connect the output port of the **Two-Class Bayes Point Machine** module to the first input port of the **Train Model** module. Connect the first output port of the **Split** module to the second input of the **Train Model** module. In the properties pane for the **Train Model** module, click on the **Launch column selector** button and when the pop-up appears, set **Class variable (0 or 1)** as the column's target variable, as shown in the following screenshot:

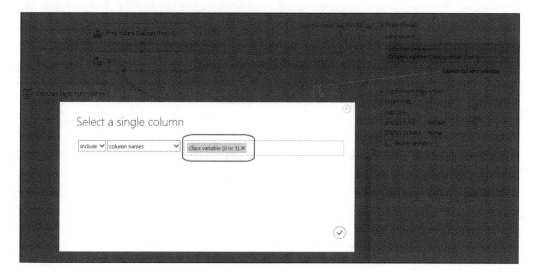

Next, drag the **Score Model** and **Evaluate Model** modules to the canvas. Connect the output of the **Train Model** module to the first input of the **Score Model** module and the second output of the **Split** module to the second input of the **Score Model** module. Then, connect the output of the **Score Model** module to the first input of the **Evaluate Model** module. Let's take a look at the following screenshot:

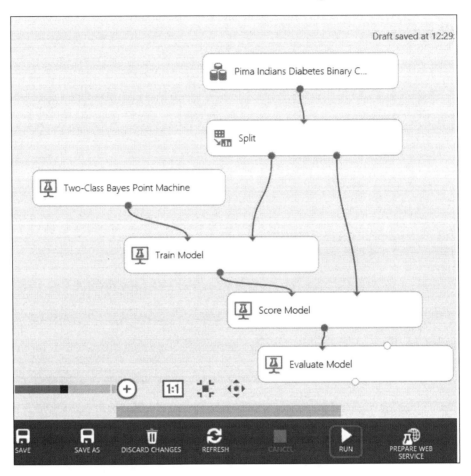

Click on **RUN** and run the experiment. When it finishes (after all the modules gets a green tick mark), right-click on the output of the **Evaluate Model** module and click on the **Visualize** option to view the **Evaluation Results**, as shown in the following screenshot:

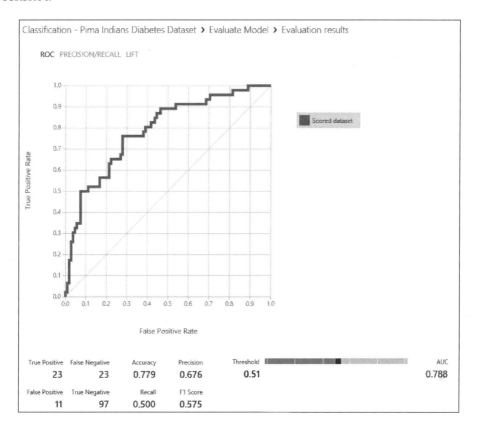

By default, the graph shows the ROC curve. The more area it covers, the better the model performs. This is represented by the matric AUC. AUC, as you can find here, is **0.788**.

Note the **Threshold** scrollbar, which is set to **0.51** at the moment, which is **0.5** by default. You can increase or decrease it by dragging it to the left or right. As you change the value of threshold, all the other metrics apart from AUC get changed. The reason is obvious because when there are changes to the value of true positive and true negative, the rest of the values change. At the current value, the **Threshold (0.51) Accuracy** option is set at **77.9** percent.

You can also view the graph for precision/recall and lift by clicking on the respective tab at the top-left corner of the screen.

# Two-class neural network with parameter sweeping

We will use the same diabetes dataset that we used to build the model using the neural network and to tune the parameter by parameter sweeping.

Create a new experiment. Drag and connect the same dataset to the **Split** module, as you did in the previous section. Set **0.8** as the parameter; **Fraction of rows** in the first output dataset is split into 80-20 to get your train and test dataset, respectively.

Type Sweep in the search box in the modules palette to the left of the screen and when the **Sweep Parameters** module appears, drag it to the canvas. Then, join the first output of the **Split** module to the second input of the **Sweep Parameters** module and join the second output of the **Split** module to the third input of the **Sweep Parameters** module. Let's take a look at the following screenshot:

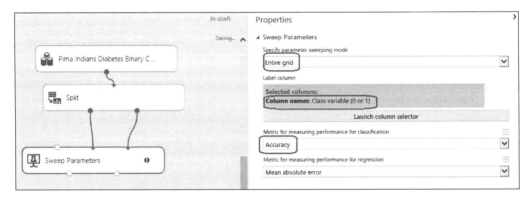

Now, you need to set the column of the dataset that is your target or label or class column for which you will train a model to make a prediction. In this case, **Class variable (0 or 1)** is the target variable or class for which you are going to make a prediction. Also, set the sweeping mode to **Entire grid** and **Metric for measure the performance for Classification** to **Accuracy**. Ignore the other parameter as this is a classification problem.

Type Two-Class Neural Network in search box at the top of the modules palette to the left and drag the **Two-Class Neural Network** module to the canvas. Connect it to the first input of the **Sweep Parameters** module. As usual, drag the **Score Model** and **Evaluate Model** modules to the canvas and make the necessary connections.

Connect the second output port of the **Sweep Parameters** module to the first input port of the **Score Model** module and connect the second output of the **Split** module to the second input of the **Score Model** module. Then, connect the output of the **Score Model** module to the first input of the **Evaluate Model** module.

Run the experiment. Let's take a look at the following screenshot:

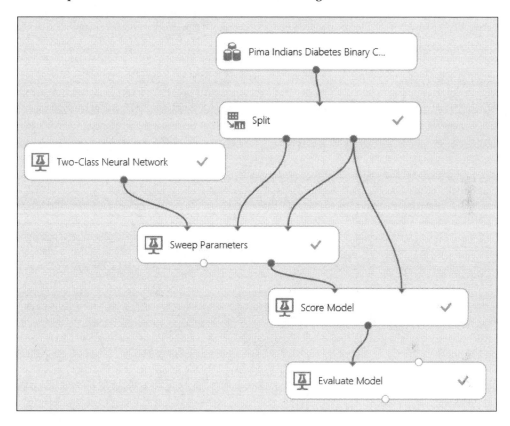

As the experiment finishes running, visualize the output of the **Evaluate Model** module to measure the performance of the model. Note the AUC and accuracy metrics.

While using parameter sweeping to find the best parameters for the model, it is a good practice to use a separate dataset to score and evaluate the prediction than what is used for training and parameter tuning. To illustrate the point, you can split your dataset into 60 percent and 40 percent. Then, use another split module to split the 40 percent (the second dataset) into 50 percent each. So now, you have three datasets containing 60 percent, 20 percent, and 20 percent of your original dataset. Then, use the first 60 percent and 20 percent for the **Sweep Parameters** module and the rest 20 percent for scoring and evaluation. Let's take a look at the following screenshot:

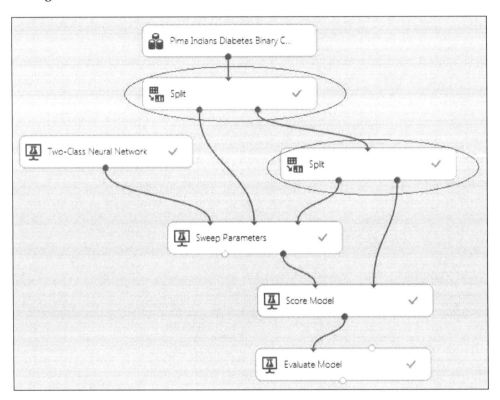

# Predicting adult income with decision-tree-based models

ML Studio comes with three decision-tree-based algorithms for two-class classification: the **Two-Class Decision Forest**, **Two-Class Boosted Decision Tree**, and **Two-Class Decision Jungle** modules. These are known as ensemble models where more than one decision trees are assembled to obtain better predictive performance. Though all the three are based on decision trees, their underlying algorithms differ.

We will first build a model with the **Two-Class Decision Forest** module and then compare it with the **Two-Class Boosted Decision Tree** module for the **Adult Census Income Binary Classification dataset** module, which is one of the sample datasets available in ML Studio. The dataset is a subset of the 1994 US census database and contains the demographic information of working adults over the 16 years age limit. Each instance or example in the dataset has a label or class variable that states whether a person earns 50K a year or not.

Create an experiment and drag the dataset from the **Saved Datasets** group in the module palette. Right-click on the output port and click on **Visualize** to explore the dataset. When you click on the different columns, you can find that these columns contain a large number of missing values: **workclass**, **occupation**, and **native-country**. Other columns don't have missing values. Let's take a look at the following screenshot:

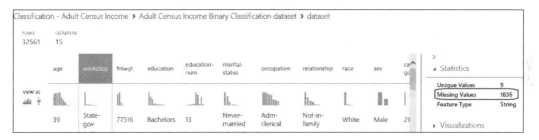

Though it would still work, if you still build models with missing values, we would get rid of these columns in our models. Missing values may impact the predicted result.

In the search box, type `Project` and drag the **Project Columns** module to the canvas. Connect the dataset module to this module. On the properties pane, click on the **Launch Column Selector** module, so that the pop-up columns selector comes up. As you can see in the following screenshot, begin with all the columns and exclude the columns with the missing values: **workclass**, **occupation**, and **native-country**:

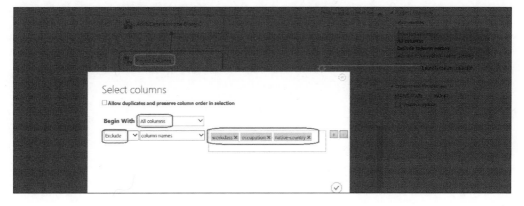

Expand the **Data Transformation** group and then expand the **Sample and Split** option in the modules palette and drag the **Split** module to the canvas. Set the **Fraction of rows** parameter in the first output dataset to **0.8** and leave the others at their default values. You are splitting the dataset so that 80 percent of the data will be used to train and rest 20 percent will be used for test.

Likewise, now drag the **Two-Class Decision Forest** module to the canvas. Type Decision Forest in the search box in the modules palette to the left and when the module appears, drag it to the canvas. Set the **Resampling method** property to **Bagging** and leave the rest of the parameters at their default values. Leave the module with the default values for the properties.

Drag a **Train Model** module to the canvas and connect the output port of the **Two-Class Decision Forest** module to the first input port of the **Train Model** module. Connect the first output port of the **Split** module to the second input of the **Train Model** module. In the properties pane for the **Train** module, click on the **column selector** option and set **income** as the column's target variable.

Next, drag the **Score Model** and **Evaluate Model** modules to the canvas. Connect the output of the **Train Model** module to the first input of the **Score Model** module and connect the second output of the **Split** module to the second input of the **Score Model** module. Then, connect the output of the **Score Model** module to the first input of the **Evaluate Model** module.

Run the experiment and after its successful execution, visualize the evaluation result. Let's take a look at the following screenshot:

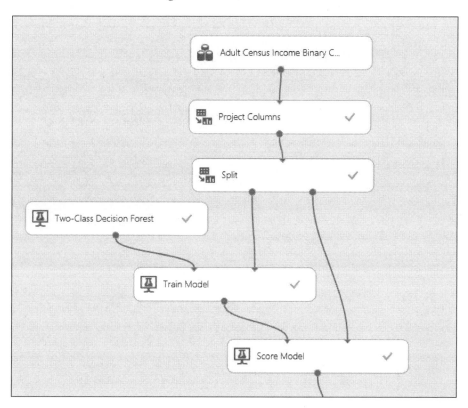

As with any experiment, you can now compare your model with another algorithm. You built a model using the **Two-Class Decision Forest** module. Now, use another algorithm, such as the **Two-Class Boosted Decision Tree** module and evaluate it.

To do so, start with the experiment and select the **Train** and **Score** modules by pressing *ctrl* on your keyboard and clicking on both the modules. Then, copy the selected modules and paste them on the canvas by right-clicking on them and pasting them or just by pressing *ctrl + v* on your keyboard. It supports copy paste much like any other MS product, for example, MS Word.

Now, click anywhere on the canvas to unselect the pasted modules and rearrange them so that no module is placed on another and all are readable. Remove the connection between the **Two-Class Decision Forest** and the **Train Model** modules by selecting them and pressing *Delete*. Drag the **Two-Class Boosted Decision Tree** module from the left-hand side palette, to the canvas and connect the output of the module to the **Train Model** module. Leave it at the default property values. Connect the output of the **Score Model** module to the second input of the **Evaluate Model** module and run the experiment. Let's take a look at the following screenshot:

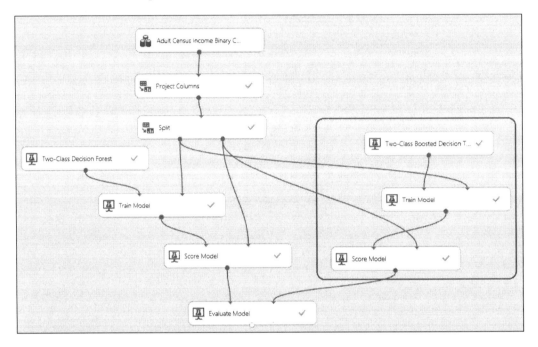

After the successful run, right-click on the output port of the **Evaluate Model** module and click on **Visualize** to find the evaluation result of the two models on a single canvas.

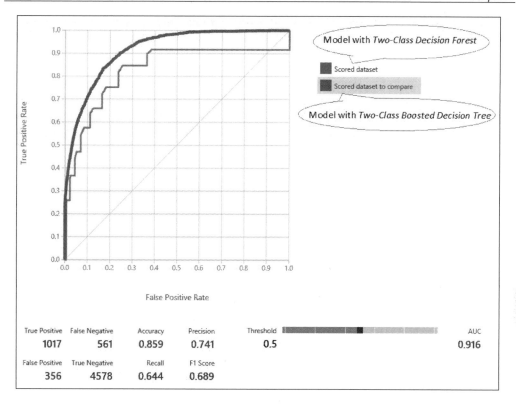

As you can see in the preceding graph, with the current settings, the model with the **Two-Class Boosted Decision Tree** module has higher values than the other when you see the AUC and accuracy figures.

So, we know that it is performing better than the other one.

# Do it yourself – comparing models to choose the best

You have already tried two algorithms for the **Adult Census Income Binary Classification dataset** module. Now, try another two modules to choose the best one for your final model: the **Two-Class Boosted Decision Tree** and the **Two-Class Neural Network** modules. Try out different parameters; use the **Sweep Parameters** module to optimize the parameters for the algorithms. The following screenshot is just for your reference—your experiment might differ. You may also try this with other available algorithms, for example, the **Two-Class Averaged Perceptron** or the **Two-Class Logistic Regression** modules to find the best model. Let's take a look at the following screenshot:

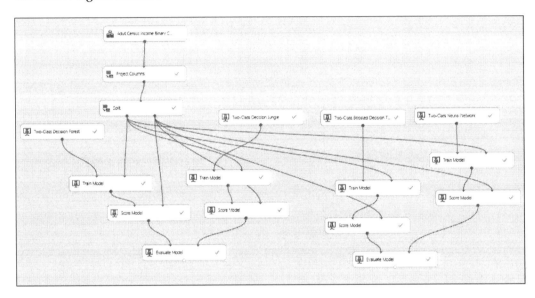

# Multiclass classification

The classification you have seen and experienced so far is a two-class classification where the target variable can be of two classes. In multiclass classification, you classify in more than two classes, for example continuing on our hypothetical tumor problem, for a given tumor size and age of a patient, you might predict one of these three classes as the possibility of a patient being affected with cancer: High, Medium, and Low. In theory, a target variable can have any number of classes.

# Evaluation metrics – multiclass classification

ML Studio lets you evaluate your model with an accuracy that is calculated as a ratio of the number of correct predictions versus the incorrect ones. Consider the following table:

| Age | Tumor size | Actual class | Predicted class |
|-----|-----------|--------------|-----------------|
| 32 | 135 | Low | Medium |
| 47 | 121 | Medium | Medium |
| 28 | 156 | Medium | High |
| 45 | 162 | High | High |
| 77 | 107 | Medium | Medium |

The following can be the evaluation metrics where in the columns, the text is marked in bold and have background colors according to the accuracy per class. For example, there were three actual classes as Medium, but only two were correctly predicted, so *accuracy = 2/3 = 66.6 %*. It also shows that 33.3 percent of the Medium class was inaccurately predicted as High. This is also known as the confusion matrix. Let's take a look at the following table:

| Predicted Actual | Low | Medium | High |
|------------------|-----|--------|------|
| **Low** | 0 (0 percent) | 1 (100 percent) | |
| **Medium** | | 2 (66.6 percent) | 1(33.3 percent) |
| **High** | | | 1 (100 percent) |

# Multiclass classification with the Iris dataset

The **Iris** dataset is one of the classic and simple datasets. It contains the observations about the Iris plant. Each instance has four features: the sepal length, sepal width, petal length, and petal width. All the measurements are in centimeters. The dataset contains three classes for the target variable, where each class refers to a type of Iris plant: **Iris Setosa**, **Iris Versicolour**, and **Iris Virginica**.

You can find more information on this dataset at `http://archive.ics.uci.edu/ml/datasets/Iris`.

As this dataset is not present as a sample dataset in ML Studio, you need to import it to ML Studio using a reader module before building any model on it. Note that the **Iris dataset** present in the **Saved Dataset** section is the subset of the original dataset and is only present for two classes.

# Multiclass decision forest

Decision forest is also available for multiclass classification. We will first use this with parameter sweep to train the model.

Follow the given steps to import the Iris dataset:

1.  Go to ML Studio. Click on the **+NEW** button and choose **Blank Experiment**.

2.  From the modules palette, find the **Reader** module under the **Data Input and Output** group and drag it to the experiment canvas.

3.  The module properties pane is displayed after this. Choose the data source as **HTTP**.

4.  Specify a complete URL: `http://archive.ics.uci.edu/ml/machine-learning-databases/iris/iris.data`.

5.  Specify the data format as **CSV**.

6.  Don't tick the checkbox for the header row, as the dataset does not contain any header. You might end up with something as follows:

Run the experiment and when you see the green tick mark on the **Reader** module, right-click on the output port and click on **Visualize**. Clicking on any column, you can notice that ML Studio shows a missing value.

Use the **Clean Missing Data** module to remove the row containing the missing value. Drag the module that can be found under the **Data Transformation** group and then under **Manipulation** in the modules palette to the canvas. Connect the output port of the **Reader** module to the input port of this module. On the properties pane, choose **Remove entire row** for the property for **Cleaning mode**, as shown in the following screenshot:

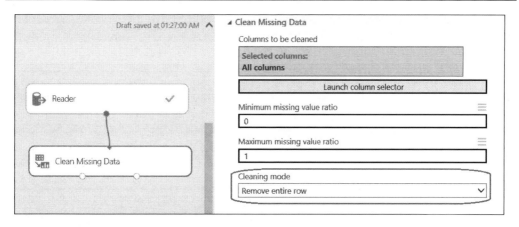

Expand the **Data Transformation** group and then expand the **Sample and Split** option in the modules palette and drag the **Split** module to the canvas. Set the **Fraction of rows** parameter in the first output dataset to **0.7** and leave the others at their default values. You are splitting the dataset so that 70 percent of the data will be used to train and the other 30 percent will be used for test.

Likewise, now drag the **Multiclass Decision Forest** module to canvas. To do so, type Decision Forest in the search box in the modules palette to the left and when the module appears, drag it to the canvas. Set the **Resampling method** property to **Bagging** and leave the rest of the properties at their default values. Leave the module with the default values for the properties.

Drag a **Train Model** module to the canvas and connect the output port of the **Multiclass Decision Forest** module to the first input port of the **Train Model** module. Connect the first output port of the **Split** module to the second input of the **Train Medel** module. In the properties pane for the **Train Model** module, click on the column selector and set **Col5** as the column's target variable.

Next, drag the **Score Model** and **Evaluate Model** modules to the canvas. Connect the output of the **Train Model** module to the first input of the **Score Model** module and connect the second output of the **Split** module to the second input of the **Score Model** module. Then, connect the output of the **Score Model** module to the first input of the **Evaluate Model** module. Let's take a look at the following screenshot:

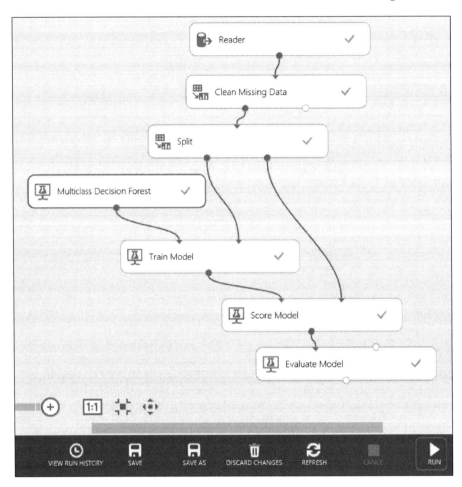

Now, run the experiment and after its completion, visualize the output of the **Evaluate Model** module to know the performance of the model.

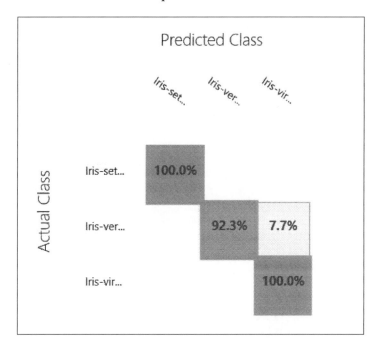

As you can see in the preceding graph, the **Iris Versicolour** class has **92.3%** accuracy, while others have **100%**. Also, **7.7%** of the time the **Iris Versicolour** class has been misclassified as **Iris Virginica**.

Note that you have not done any optimization by tuning the parameters. You can try out different values for the parameters and evaluate the performance or simply use the **Sweep Parameters** module to get the best parameters.

# Comparing models – multiclass decision forest and logistic regression

As with any experiment, you can now compare your model with another algorithm. You built a model using multiclass decision forest. Now, use another algorithm, such as multiclass logistic regression to evaluate the prediction.

To do so, start with the experiment and select the **Train** and **Score** modules by pressing *ctrl* on your keyboard and click on both the modules. Then, copy the selected modules and paste them on the canvas by right-clicking on it and pasting them or just by pressing *ctrl + v* on your keyboard. Now, click anywhere on the canvas to unselect the pasted modules and rearrange them so that no module is placed on another and all are readable. Let's take a look at the following screenshot:

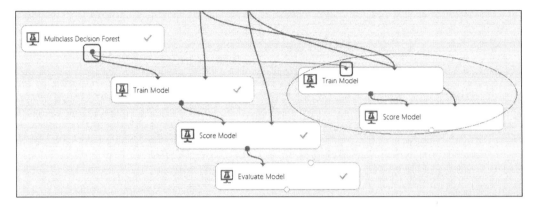

Now, remove the connection between the **Multiclass Decision Forest** and **Train Model** modules by selecting the connection and pressing *Delete*. Note the connection in the preceding screenshot. Drag the **Multiclass Logistic Regression** module from the left-hand side palette to the canvas and connect the output of the module to the **Train Model** module. Leave the properties of the **Multiclass Logistic Regression** module at their default values. Connect the output of the **Score Model** module to the second input of the **Evaluate Model** module. Let's take a look at the following screenshot:

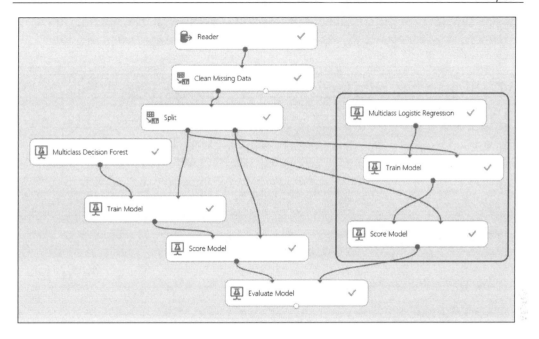

You can run the model to find out how the new model is performing and then you can compare the evaluation metrics. After the experiment finishes running, visualize the output of the **Evaluate Model** module to know the performance of the model.

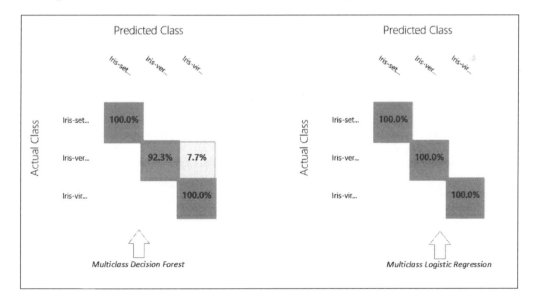

As you can note, for the model with the logistic regression, you are getting **100%** accuracy for all the classes. Given such a scenario, you know which model to pick up.

# Multiclass classification with the Wine dataset

The **Wine** dataset is another classic and simple dataset hosted in the UCI machine learning repository. It contains chemical analysis of the content of wines grown in the same region in Italy, but derived from three different cultivars. It is used to determine models for classification problems by predicting the source (cultivar) of wine as class or target variable. The dataset has the following 13 features (dependent variables), which are all numeric:

- Alcohol
- Malic acid
- Ash
- Alcalinity of ash
- Magnesium
- Total phenols
- Flavanoids
- Nonflavanoid phenols
- Proanthocyanins
- Color intensity
- Hue
- OD280/OD315 of diluted wines
- Proline

The examples or instances are classified into three classes: 1, 2 and 3.

You can find more about the dataset at `http://archive.ics.uci.edu/ml/datasets/Wine`.

# Multiclass neural network with parameter sweep

We will build a model with multiclass neural network and optimize the parameters with the **Sweep Parameter** module.

As you did the last time, use the **Reader** module to import the dataset from `http://archive.ics.uci.edu/ml/machine-learning-databases/wine/wine.data`.

It is in the CSV format and has no header row, as shown in the following screenshot:

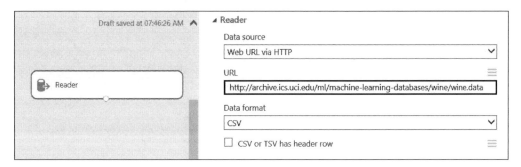

Use the **Split** module and split it into the ratio of 70:30 for a train and test dataset, respectively.

Type `Sweep` in the search box in the modules palette to the left and when the **Sweep Parameters** module appears, drag it to the canvas. Then, join the first output of the **Split** module to the second input of the **Sweep Parameters** module and join the second output of the **Split** module to the third input of the **Sweep Parameters** module.

Now, you need to set the column of the dataset that is your target, label, or class column for which you will train a model to make a prediction. In this case, **Col1** is the target variable or class for which you are going to make a prediction. Also, set the sweeping mode to **Entire grid** for metric to measure the performance of the **Classification to Accuracy** option.

Also, get the **Multiclass Neural Network** module and connect it to the first input of the **Sweep Parameters** module. As usual, drag the **Score Model** and **Evaluate Model** modules to the canvas. Connect the second output port of the **Sweep Parameters** module to the first input port of the **Score Model** module and connect the second output of the **Split** module to the second input of the **Score Model** module. Then, connect the output of the **Score Model** module to the first input of the **Evaluate Model** module.

Run the experiment.

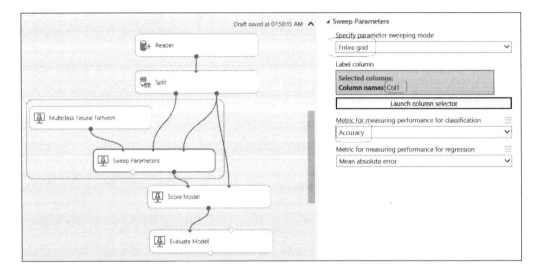

As the experiment finishes running, visualize the output of the **Evaluate Model** module to know the performance of the model.

# Do it yourself – multiclass decision jungle

Use the same Wine dataset and build a model using the **Multiclass Decision Jungle** module. You can use the Sweep Parameters module to optimize the parameters of the algorithms. After you run the experiment, check out the evaluation metrics. Do you find any improvement in the performance than the previous model you built with neural network or any other available algorithms?

# Summary

You started the chapter with understanding predictive analysis with classification and explored the concepts of training, testing, and validating a classification model. You then proceeded to carry on building experiments with different two-class and multiclass classification models, such as logistic regression, decision forest, neural network, and boosted decision trees inside ML Studio. You learned how to score and evaluate a model after training. You also learned how to optimize different parameters for a learning algorithm by the module, Sweep Parameters.

After exploring the two-class classification, you understood multiclass classification and learnt how to evaluate a model for the same. You then built a couple of models for multiclass classification using different available algorithms.

In the next chapter, you will explore the process of building a model using clustering, an unsupervised learning algorithm.

# 8
# Clustering

Birds of a feather flock together—clustering is all about this. It's an unsupervised learning where the class or label is not known. So, you get a dataset and then with the algorithm, you divide and group the instances into different clusters with an objective of keeping all the similar ones together.

Clustering has many different application areas, such as customer segmentation, social network analysis, computational biology, and many more.

In this chapter, you will start with understanding the **K-means clustering** algorithm and then, you will learn how to build a model using this in ML Studio.

## Understanding the K-means clustering algorithm

The K-means clustering algorithm is the most popular clustering algorithm. It is simple and powerful. As the name suggests, the algorithm creates K clusters out of the dataset where $K$ is a number you decide. For simplicity, let's consider a dataset with two features and let's plot them on a two dimensional space as one feature on $x$ axis and the other on $y$ axis. Again, note that as clustering is an unsupervised learning problem, no label, class, or dependent variable is required.

With the K-means algorithm, K centroids are determined for K clusters. All the points in a cluster are closest to its centroid than to any other centroids.

Consider $K = 3$, where there are 3 clusters and hence 3 centroids, as you can find in the following figure. So by intuition, take any point and calculate its distance from the three centroids. The point will belong to the cluster whose centroid is the nearest.

For a point, let $d1$ be the distance from Centroid 1, $d2$ be the distance from Centroid 2, and $d3$ be the distance from Centroid 3.

If *d2* < *d1* and *d2* < *d3*, then the point closest to centroid 2 belongs to the cluster 2. Let's take a look at the following diagram:

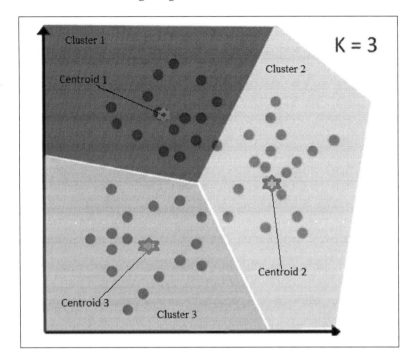

# Creating a K-means clustering model using ML Studio

Now, it's time for you to build a clustering model by yourself. ML Studio comes with two modules specific for K-means clustering.

The URL `http://www.biz.uiowa.edu/faculty/jledolter/DataMining/protein.csv` contains a dataset in CSV format.

It contains the protein intakes of 9 different food sources from 25 European countries. The first few instances in the dataset are listed as follows:

| Country | RedMeat | WhiteMeat | Eggs | Milk | Fish | Cereals | Starch | Nuts | Fr&Veg |
|---------|---------|-----------|------|------|------|---------|--------|------|--------|
| Albania | 10.1 | 1.4 | 0.5 | 8.9 | 0.2 | 42.3 | 0.6 | 5.5 | 1.7 |
| Austria | 8.9 | 14 | 4.3 | 19.9 | 2.1 | 28 | 3.6 | 1.3 | 4.3 |
| Belgium | 13.5 | 9.3 | 4.1 | 17.5 | 4.5 | 26.6 | 5.7 | 2.1 | 4 |
| Bulgaria | 7.8 | 6 | 1.6 | 8.3 | 1.2 | 56.7 | 1.1 | 3.7 | 4.2 |
| Czechoslovakia | 9.7 | 11.4 | 2.8 | 12.5 | 2 | 34.3 | 5 | 1.1 | 4 |
| Denmark | 10.6 | 10.8 | 3.7 | 25 | 9.9 | 21.9 | 4.8 | 0.7 | 2.4 |
| E Germany | 8.4 | 11.6 | 3.7 | 11.1 | 5.4 | 24.6 | 6.5 | 0.8 | 3.6 |
| Finland | 9.5 | 4.9 | 2.7 | 33.7 | 5.8 | 26.3 | 5.1 | 1 | 1.4 |
| France | 18 | 9.9 | 3.3 | 19.5 | 5.7 | 28.1 | 4.8 | 2.4 | 6.5 |

Let's build a clustering model to group the dataset into three clusters based on the protein intakes of different countries from a variety of sources.

Create a new experiment and drag the **Reader** module under the **Data Input and Output** section in the modules palette to the left of the canvas. On the properties pane to the right, choose **Data Source** as **Web URL via HTTP**, **Data format** as **CSV**, and tick the checkbox for **CSV or TSV has header row**. Also, on the URL textbox, add the previously mentioned URL to the CSV file.

Drag the **K-Means Clustering** module to the canvas. This module is for the algorithm. As you need three clusters for your dataset, set the **Number of Centroids** option to **3** in the properties pane and leave the others with their default parameters, as shown in the following screenshot:

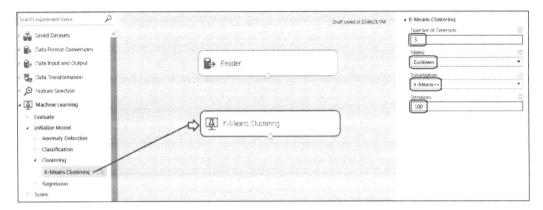

Drag the **Train Clustering Model** module to the canvas and make a connection, as shown in the following screenshot. For the **Country** column in the dataset, your target is to make the algorithm work based on the protein intakes. So, exclude the column and include everything else.

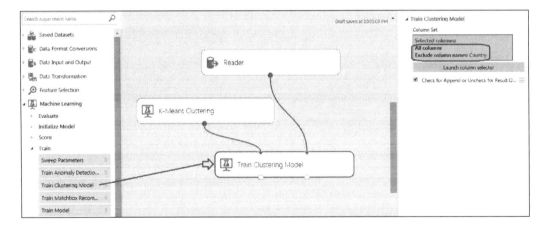

Drag the **Assign to Clusters** module to the canvas and make a connection, as shown in the following screenshot. Exclude the **Country** column and include everything else.

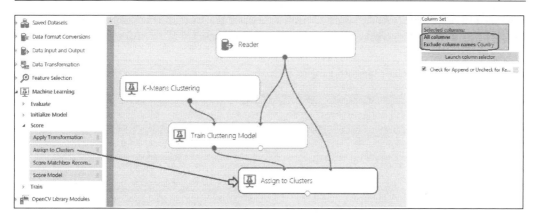

Now, drag a **Project Columns** module and connect the output of the **Assign to Clusters** module to its input. Select **All columns** by clicking on the **Launch column selector** option in the properties pane for the module, as shown in the following screenshot:

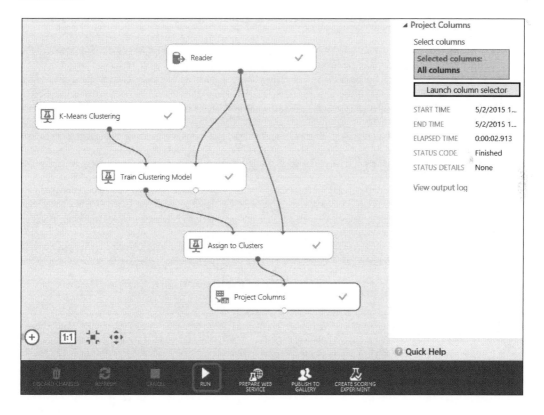

Run the experiment and right-click on the output port of the **Project Columns** module and visualize the output with the clusters assigned as follows:

| Country | RedMeat | WhiteMeat | Eggs | Milk | Fish | Cereals | Starch | Nuts | Fr&Veg | Assignments |
|---|---|---|---|---|---|---|---|---|---|---|
| Albania | 10.1 | 1.4 | 0.5 | 8.9 | 0.2 | 42.3 | 0.6 | 5.5 | 1.7 | 0 |
| Austria | 8.9 | 14 | 4.3 | 19.9 | 2.1 | 28 | 3.6 | 1.3 | 4.3 | 1 |
| Belgium | 13.5 | 9.3 | 4.1 | 17.5 | 4.5 | 26.6 | 5.7 | 2.1 | 4 | 1 |
| Bulgaria | 7.8 | 6 | 1.6 | 8.3 | 1.2 | 56.7 | 1.1 | 3.7 | 4.2 | 0 |
| Czechoslovakia | 9.7 | 11.4 | 2.8 | 12.5 | 2 | 34.3 | 5 | 1.1 | 4 | 2 |
| Denmark | 10.6 | 10.8 | 3.7 | 25 | 9.9 | 21.9 | 4.8 | 0.7 | 2.4 | 1 |
| E Germany | 8.4 | 11.6 | 3.7 | 11.1 | 5.4 | 24.6 | 6.5 | 0.8 | 3.6 | 2 |
| Finland | 9.5 | 4.9 | 2.7 | 33.7 | 5.8 | 26.3 | 5.1 | 1 | 1.4 | 1 |
| France | 18 | 9.9 | 3.3 | 19.5 | 5.7 | 28.1 | 4.8 | 2.4 | 6.5 | 1 |
| Greece | 10.2 | 3 | 2.8 | 17.6 | 5.9 | 41.7 | 2.2 | 7.8 | 6.5 | 0 |
| Hungary | 5.3 | 12.4 | 2.9 | 9.7 | 0.3 | 40.1 | 4 | 5.4 | 4.2 | 2 |

The output table has the rightmost **Assignments** column that contains the cluster (number) assigned to each cluster. As you can see, we've found that different countries fall into one of the three clusters based on the protein intakes, for example, **Czechoslovakia** belongs to cluster 2 and **France** to cluster 1.

Here, you've found the clusters for the same training data. However, after training, you can find the clusters for new datasets as well.

# Do it yourself

There is a sample dataset under the **Saved Datasets** option in ML Studio called **Iris Two Class Data**. Use this to build a **K-Means Clustering** model with $K$ (*Number of Centroids*) = 2.

This is not a test, but did you notice that all the instances of one class fall in the same cluster? Don't be confused between the cluster number as *0* and *1* because it is just a number and it won't harm even if you read the cluster 0 as 1 and *1* as *0*.

# Clustering versus classification

It might be confusing for beginners to distinguish between a clustering problem and a classification problem. Classification is fundamentally different from clustering. Classification is a supervised learning problem where your class or target variable is known to train a dataset. The algorithm is trained to look at the examples (features and class or target variables) and then you score and test it with a test dataset.

Clustering, being an unsupervised learning, it works on a dataset with no label or class variable. Also, you don't perform scoring and testing with a test dataset. So, you just apply your algorithm to your data and group them into a different cluster, say 1, 2 and 3, which were not known before.

So, to put it simply, if you have a dataset and a class/label or target variable as categorical variable and you have to predict the target variable for a new dataset based on the given dataset, it's a classification problem. If you are just given a dataset with no label or target variable and you just have to group them into $n$ clusters, then it's a clustering case.

# Summary

After a quick overview of the unsupervised learning, you proceeded to understand clustering and the K-means clustering algorithm. Then, you built a clustering model using ML Studio and learned about three modules for K-means clustering.

In the next chapter, you will explore the Recommender System and learn to build a simple model for the same.

# A Recommender System

# 9

Recommender systems are common these days. You may not have noticed, but you might already be a user or receiver of such a system somewhere. Most of the well-performing e-commerce platforms use recommendation systems to recommend items to their users. When you see on the Amazon website that a book is recommended to you based on your earlier preferences, purchases, and browse history, Amazon is actually using such a recommendation system. Similarly, Netflix uses its recommendation system to suggest movies for you.

A recommender or recommendation system is used to recommend a product or information often based on user characteristics, preferences, history, and so on. So, a recommendation is always personalized.

Until recently, it was not so easy or straightforward to build a recommender, but Azure ML makes it really easy to build one as long as you have your data ready.

This chapter introduces you to the concept of recommendation systems and also the model available in ML Studio for you to build your own recommender system. It then walks you through the process of building a recommendation system with a simple example.

## The Matchbox recommender

Microsoft has developed a large-scale recommender system based on a probabilistic model (Bayesian) called **Matchbox**. This model can learn about a user's preferences through observations made on how they rate items, such as movies, content, or other products. Based on those observations, it recommends new items to the users when requested.

Matchbox uses the available data for each user in the most efficient way possible. The learning algorithm it uses is designed specifically for big data. However, its main feature is that Matchbox takes advantage of metadata available for both users and items. This means that the things it learns about one user or item can be transferred across to other users or items.

You can find more information about the Matchbox model at the Microsoft Research project link.

# Types of recommendations

The Matchbox recommender supports the building of four kinds of recommenders, which will include most of the scenarios. Let's take a look at the following list:

- **Rating Prediction**: This predicts ratings for a given user and item, for example, if a new movie is released, the system will predict what will be your rating for that movie out of 1-5.

- **Item Recommendation**: This recommends items to a given user, for example, Amazon suggests you books or YouTube suggests you videos to watch on its home page (especially when you are logged in).

- **Related Users**: This finds users that are related to a given user, for example, LinkedIn suggests people that you can get connected to or Facebook suggests friends to you.

- **Related Items**: This finds the items related to a given item, for example, a blog site suggests you related posts when you are reading a blog post.

# Understanding the recommender modules

The Matchbox recommender comes with three components; as you might have guessed, a module each to train, score, and evaluate the data. The modules are described as follows.

# The Train Matchbox recommender

This module contains the algorithm and generates the trained algorithm, as shown in the following screenshot:

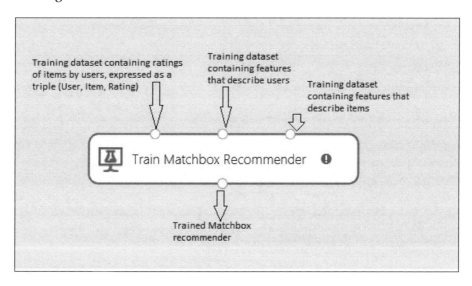

This module takes the values for the following two parameters.

## The number of traits

This value decides how many implicit features (traits) the algorithm will learn about that are related to every user and item. The higher this value, the precise it would be as it would lead to better prediction. Typically, it takes a value in the range of 2 to 20.

## The number of recommendation algorithm iterations

It is the number of times the algorithm iterates over the data. The higher this value, the better would the predictions be. Typically, it takes a value in the range of 1 to 10.

# The Score Matchbox recommender

This module lets you specify the kind of recommendation and corresponding parameters you want:

- Rating Prediction
- Item Prediction
- Related Users
- Related Items

Let's take a look at the following screenshot:

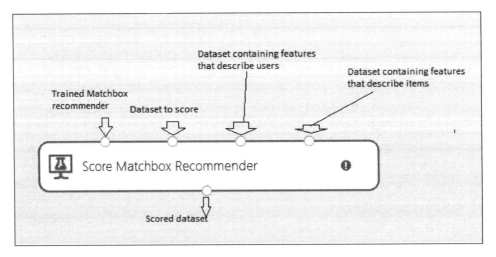

The ML Studio help page for the module provides details of all the corresponding parameters.

## The evaluate recommender

This module takes a test and a scored dataset and generates evaluation metrics, as shown in the following screenshot:

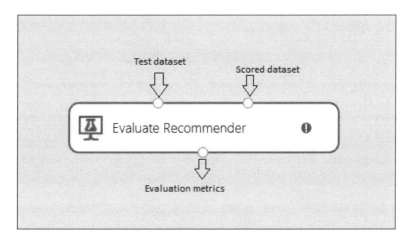

It also lets you specify the kind of recommendation, such as the score module and corresponding parameters.

# Building a recommendation system

Now, it would be worthwhile that you learn to build one by yourself. We will build a simple recommender system to recommend restaurants to a given user.

ML Studio includes three sample datasets, described as follows:

- **Restaurant customer data**: This is a set of metadata about customers, including demographics and preferences, for example, **latitude**, **longitude**, **interest**, and **personality**.

- **Restaurant feature data**: This is a set of metadata about restaurants and their features, such as food type, dining style, and location, for example, **placeID**, **latitude**, **longitude**, **price**.

- **Restaurant ratings**: This contains the ratings given by users to restaurants on a scale of 0 to 2. It contains the columns: **userID**, **placeID**, and **rating**.

Now, we will build a recommender that will recommend a given number of restaurants to a user (**userID**). To build a recommender perform the following steps:

1. Create a new experiment. In the Search box in the modules palette, type `Restaurant`. The preceding three datasets get listed. Drag them all to the canvas one after another.

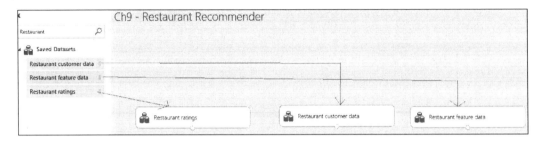

2. Drag a **Split** module and connect it to the output port of the **Restaurant ratings** module. On the properties section to the right, choose **Splitting mode** as **Recommender Split**. Leave the other parameters at their default values.

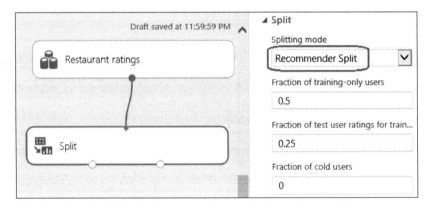

3. Drag a **Project Columns** module to the canvas and select the columns: **userID**, **latitude**, **longitude**, **interest**, and **personality**.

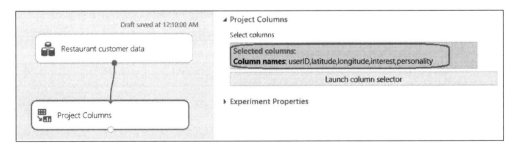

4. Similarly, drag another **Project Columns** module and connect it to the **Restaurant feature data** module and select the columns: **placeID**, **latitude**, **longitude**, **price**, **the_geom_meter**, and **address**, **zip**.

5. Drag a **Train Matchbox Recommender** module to the canvas and make connections to the three input ports, as shown in the following screenshot:

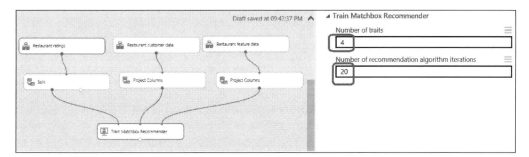

6. Drag a **Score Matchbox Recommender** module to the canvas and make connections to the three input ports and set the property's values, as shown in the following screenshot:

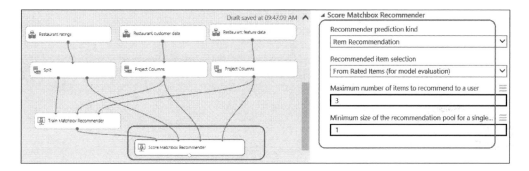

7.  Run the experiment and when it gets completed, right-click on the output
    of the **Score Matchbox Recommender** module and click on **Visualize** to
    explore the scored data.

| view as | User | Item 1 | Item 2 | Item 3 |
|---|---|---|---|---|
| | U1048 | 135034 | 135026 | 135065 |
| | U1117 | 135018 | 132766 | 135088 |
| | U1049 | 135052 | 132862 | 135051 |
| | U1088 | 135057 | 135071 | 135032 |
| | U1062 | 135052 | 135045 | 135062 |
| | U1035 | 134986 | 135018 | 132773 |
| | U1125 | 135062 | 135076 | 135038 |
| | U1013 | 135075 | 135079 | 132921 |

You can note the different restaurants (IDs) recommended as items for a user
from the test dataset. The next step is to evaluate the scored prediction. Drag the
**Evaluate Recommender** module to the canvas and connect the second output of the
**Split** module to its first input port and connect the output of the **Score Matchbox
Recommender** module to its second input. Leave the module at its
default properties.

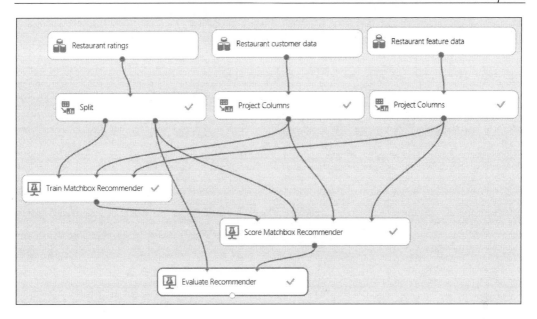

Run the experiment again and when finished, right-click on the output port of the **Evaluate Recommender** module and click on **Visualize** to find the evaluation metric.

The evaluation metric **Normalized Discounted Cumulative Gain (NDCG)** is estimated from the ground truth ratings given in the test set. Its value ranges from *0.0* to *1.0*, where *1.0* represents the most ideal ranking of the entities.

# Summary

You started with gaining the basic knowledge about a recommender system. You then understood the Matchbox recommender that comes with ML Studio along with its components. You also explored different kinds of recommendations that you can make with it. Finally, you ended up building a simple recommendation system to recommend restaurants to a given user.

In the following chapter, you will explore how to extend your experiments beyond the capability of ML Studio by writing code in either R or Python.

# 10
# Extensibility with R and Python

You have already built models using ML Studio and have realized how easy and powerful it is. Despite a lot of ready-to-use modules available in ML Studio, there are still many tasks which can't be done inside ML Studio to build a required model and solve a problem at hand. Microsoft realizes this, so allows you to extend your experiments beyond the capability of ML Studio by writing code in either R or Python.

This chapter introduces you to the process of integrating your code in your experiment. You don't need any prior skills in Python or R to successfully finish this chapter. However, you can get the best out of this if you have some exposure to any of these two languages. Also, if you want to work with Azure ML at the professional level, it is highly recommended that you gain some skills either in R or Python. If you already know Python or are choosing to pick it up, then you should get exposure to Pandas library; especially, you should learn to work with the `DataFrame` module, as you would soon find out why. If you are choosing R, then `data.frame` is its default data structure and you can't miss it.

I don't recommend you to use one language over other. It is up to you to decide on one if you don't know either. The following early sections in this chapter provide you a quick introduction to both the languages in relation to Azure ML.

# Introduction to R

**R** is an open source statistical programming language and in recent years, it has been hugely popular. R has significant and vibrant communities worldwide and it is rich with libraries/packages, which get new additions every day. R is a first-class citizen in the Azure ML land, meaning that it has its native support for the language. Among many data structures, R has the `data.frame` data structure, which can be assumed to be a data table with rows and columns with column headers. Though there are differences, you can safely think of it as a dataset in ML Studio. So, whenever a dataset is passed to R code in an experiment, it implicitly gets converted to the `data.frame` data structure.

# Introduction to Python

**Python** is also an open source general-purpose, high-level programming language. This means that it allows you to perform other functions, such as web/mobile/desktop application development along with scientific, mathematical, and statistical programming. Python is very popular among developers and also among the scientific community, such as R for the statistics community. Python is also popular for tasks such as data wrangling or munging, which is loosely the process of manually converting or mapping data from one raw form to another format that allows more convenient consumption of data. For such tasks, the Pandas library in Python is very useful and is used widely. The `DataFrame` objects comes with the Pandas library and in Azure ML, Microsoft ships this library along with the base Python and other useful libraries, such as `NumPy`, `SciPy`, `Pandas`, `IPython`, `Matplotlib`, and so on. If you are already familiar with Python then it's the **Anaconda** distribution of Python 2.7.7.

The Pandas `DataFrame` object is similar to the `data.frame` data structure in R and a dataset in ML Studio.

# Why should you extend through R/Python code?

Since the introduction of this chapter, you might be wondering that if ML Studio seems so easy and complete, then why does it need extending with coding? If you are thinking so, then let me assure you that this is not the case. To produce a predictive analytics solution for the real world, what ML Studio provides out of the box is quite promising, but very limited. The following are the common scenarios when you may need to write code and integrate with ML Studio:

- There is only a limited set of algorithms available through ML Studio. If a certain algorithm is required either for prediction or evaluation, you need to code and integrate the test. For example, there is no specific algorithm available for time series analysis in ML Studio so far.

- Though there are some options available, most of the cases of ML Studio with out-of-the box modules are not sufficient to meet the need of exploration and data preparation, which includes data wrangling and data preprocessing, for example, the need to apply the wavelet transform to the data.

- Data visualization support in ML Studio is very limited and most of the data visualization requirement can't be met with it.

- When you need to develop a new kind of model all together, you could use coding to develop that and then publish it as a web API.

- To consume data from either a new source or a dataset of a different format, you need to code and consume the data inside ML Studio.

# Extending experiments using the Python language

You can extend your experiment with the Python script through the module called **Execute Python Script**. You can explore more about this module with an illustration of processing a time series dataset. ML Studio comes with a sample dataset called **Time Series Dataset** and this is a very simple time series dataset with two columns, where one represents time as an integer and the other shows the values as integers.

This illustration involves coding in Python and later coding in R, where the objective is to demonstrate how the integration of code works. Though there will be some explanation of code through embedded comments, it may not be with every detail, as it is beyond the scope of this book. If you are new to coding, then just follow the instructions to get the desired output and understand the integration.

# Understanding the Execute Python Script module

To integrate Python code with ML Studio, you should use the **Execute Python Script** module, which is the only module available for Python as of writing this book. This module has three input ports and two output ports, as shown in the following screenshot:

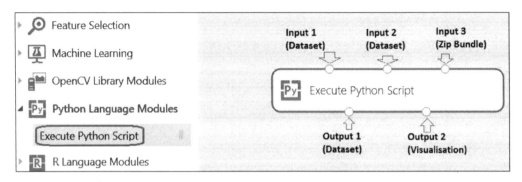

While the first two inputs are datasets, the third one expects a .zip file to be uploaded to ML Studio to import the existing code; you can find more on this in the following sub section. The first output generates a dataset that can be used further in another module and the second output is the generated visualization, Python Device, which you can only right-click on and then click on **Visualize** to view the generated graph. It supports both the console output as well as the display of PNG graphics using the Python interpreter.

The property section of the module comes with a very basic code editor, where you can write code. It also comes with a basic template of the code. The module must contain a function with the name azureml_main and it should have zero to two parameters. The function must also return a DataFrame object. Let's take a look at the following screenshot which displays the Python code which we need to integrate with the ML Studio:

```
Python script
 1  # The script MUST contain a function named azureml_main
 2  # which is the entry point for this module.
 3  #
 4  # The entry point function can contain up to two input arguments:
 5  #   Param<dataframe1>: a pandas.DataFrame
 6  #   Param<dataframe2>: a pandas.DataFrame
 7                         Input 1
 8  def azureml_main(dataframe1 = None, dataframe2 = None):
 9                                       Input 2
10  ###### Execution logic goes here ##########
11  # Code to get the result dataFrame
12      resultDataFrame = ...
13
14  # Code to generate the visualisation (if any!)
15      ...
16  # Return value must be of a sequence of pandas.DataFrame
17      return resultDataFrame,
                 Output 1
```

As you can note, the input datasets get converted to Pandas data frames. Connecting a dataset to the input ports is not a must. When an input data port is empty, the corresponding input data frame will be of the value None or null. Note here that the mapping between input ports and function parameters is positional, that is, the first connected input port, if connected, is mapped to the first parameter, **dataframe1**, of the function and the second input, if connected, is mapped to the second parameter, **dataframe2**, of the function.

You need to take care of proper indentation for Python code; otherwise, it would result in an error.

# Creating visualizations using Python

You can create data visualization using the `MatplotLib` library or any other library based on it and show it in the browser like any other visualization in ML Studio. However, the visualization created won't be automatically redirected. You have to save them as PNG files for ML Studio to pick it up and make it available through the second output port of the `Execute Python Script` module. The overall steps to generate data visualization using the `MatplotLib` library through the module are as follows:

- Change the `MatplotLib` library backend to `agg` from the default Qt-based renderer

- Create a figure using the MatplotLib API

- Get the axis and create all plots in the same axis using a MatplotLib API or any other library that uses MatplotLib as a base for plotting, for example, Pandas

- Save the generated figure to a PNG file

Now that you have an overview of how to integrate the Python code, it's time to walk you through an example.

# A simple time series analysis with the Python script

The **time series** is a sequence of data points each having a timestamp associated with it, that is usually measured over a time interval. A simple time series analysis is to find the moving average for the series.

The moving average or simple moving average can be defined as the mean of the previous $n$ number of data in a series. Here, $n$ is the window size. Consider a simple time series data, as the following, where the first column is time, the second column contains value, and the third column calculates the moving average for the window size 3. For each value, its moving average is the average of the previous three values including itself:

| Time | Value | Moving Average = Sum of previous 3 values / 3 |
|------|-------|-----------------------------------------------|
| 1 | 30 | - |
| 2 | 25 | - |
| 3 | 15 | (15+25+30)/3 = 23.3 |
| 4 | 45 | (45+15+25)/3 = 28.3 |
| 5 | 55 | (55+45+15)/3 = 38.3 |
| 6 | 5 | (5+55+45)/3 = 35.0 |
| 7 | 38 | (38+5+55)/3 = 32.7 |
| 8 | 13 | (13+38+5)/3 = 18.7 |
| 9 | 33 | (33+13+38)/3 = 28.0 |
| 10 | 31 | (31+33+13)/3 = 25.7 |

We would use the `rolling_mean` Pandas method to calculate the moving average for the window size 10 to demonstrate the Python script integration We will use the previously mentioned sample time series dataset in ML Studio, add a new column to the dataset, and assign values to it by calculating the **simple moving average** for it. Let's take a look at the following screenshot:

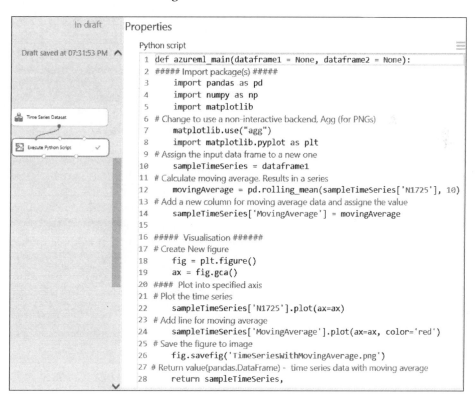

The comments in the code are self-explanatory. If you run your experiment with the preceding code, the first output will get you the modified dataset with the moving average values in the third column and the second output will get you the following visualization, where the red line represents the moving average:

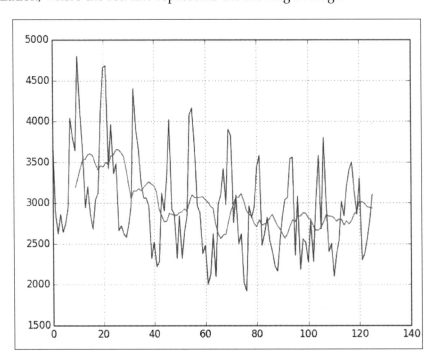

# Importing the existing Python code

It may not be always practical to write enough code in a single script box to meet the requirement. Also, there will be scenarios where you would have an already built and tested code or an external library, which you would like to use inside ML Studio. In such scenarios, you can use the third input port (Input3) of the module. You can keep the prebuilt scripts in a folder, ZIP it, and upload it to ML Studio. It will be available in the **Saved Datasets** section of the modules palette. Then, drag it to the canvas for your experiment and connect it to the third input port, Zip Bundle, of the module. The Azure ML execution framework will unzip it internally during runtime and the contents will be added to the library path of the Python interpreter. This means that the `azureml_main` entry point function can import these modules directly.

# Do it yourself – Python

Add another column to the data frame in the preceding example to moving standard deviation and plot it as another line.

 Use the moving window function `rolling_std`.

# Extending experiments using the R language

Similar to Python, you can also use the R code/script to extend your experiment inside ML Studio. However, unlike Python, you get two modules for R, which are as follows:

- **The Execute R Script module**
- **The Create R Model module**

## Understanding the Execute R Script module

Similar to the module for Python, the **Execute R Script** module also has three input ports and two output ports. The property panel for the module comes with an R script editor where you can enter your code, as shown in the following screenshot:

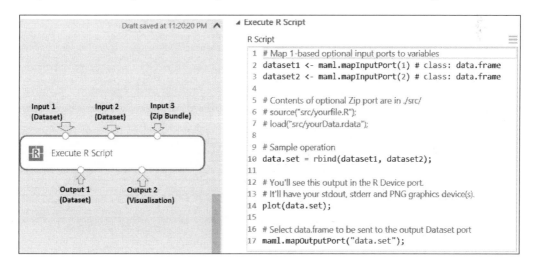

The module comes with a sample script, as you can find in the preceding screenshot. You can use the `maml.mapInputPort()` method with the port number as argument 1 for Input1, and argument 2 for Input2 to access the input dataset as an R `data.frame` object.

The third input expects a `.zip` file to be uploaded to ML Studio to import the existing code. The first output generates a dataset that can be used further in another module and the second output is the generated visualization, R Device, which you can right-click on it and then click on **Visualize** to view the generated graph. It supports the console output and the display of PNG graphics using the R interpreter. You don't have to take any extra steps to make the visualization available through the second output port of the module, as it would be redirected automatically.

Remember that if you import data that uses CSV or other formats, you have to convert the same to a dataset before using the data in an R module.

# A simple time series analysis with the R script

We will use the same time series example, as used previously, but this time, with the R script. We would use functions from an R package called **zoo**, which is already available in ML Studio. Let's take a look at the following screenshot which displays the code written in R which we are going to integrate with the ML Studio:

```
R Script
1  # Map 1-based optional input ports to variables
2  dataset1 <- maml.mapInputPort(1) # class: data.frame
3
4  # Assign input dataset to new one
5  timeSeries <- dataset1
6
7  # Load the zoo package to the session
8  library(zoo)
9
10 # Calculate moving average with moving window 10
11 ma <- rollmean(timeSeries[2],10)
12 # Add a new column and assign moving average values to it
13 timeSeries$MovingAverage[10:126] <- ma
14
15 ##### Visualisation ######
16 # Plot time series
17 plot.ts(timeSeries['N1725'], col='blue')
18 # Add a line for moving average
19 lines(timeSeries['MovingAverage'], col='red')
20
21 # Select data.frame to be sent to the output Dataset port -
22 # time series data with moving average
23 maml.mapOutputPort("timeSeries");
```

The comments in the code are self-explanatory. However, note that on the line number 13, the new column's moving average values are assigned from the position 10 and to the last position, which is 126 here. As we have taken the moving window as 10, the first nine values for the column would be null or missing.

If you run your experiment with the preceding code, the first output will get you the modified dataset with the moving average values in the third column and the second output will get you the following visualization, where the red line represents the moving average:

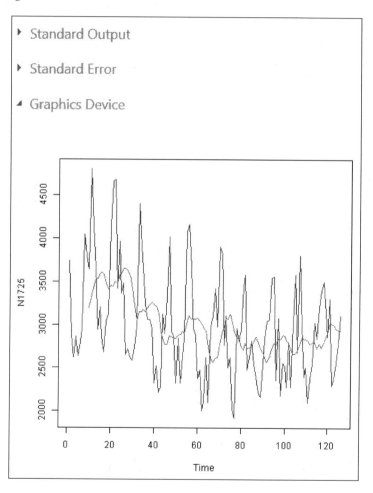

# Importing an existing R code

Like for Python, you can use the third input port (Input3) of the module to import the external code. You can keep the prebuilt scripts in a folder, ZIP it, and then upload it to ML Studio. To upload a ZIP file to your workspace, click on **New**, click on **Dataset**, and then select **From local file** and the **Zip file** option. After the upload, the zipped file will be available in the **Saved Datasets** list. Then, drag it to the canvas for your experiment and connect it to the third input port, Zip Bundle, of the module. All the files present in the ZIP file will be available for use during runtime. If any directory structure is there in the ZIP file, then it would be preserved. The root in the ZIP bundle is referred to as src.

For example, if you have created an R file named myExternalCode.R, zipped it to a file, and uploaded to ML Studio, then you can access it from the script editor for the module, shown as follows:

```
source("src/myExternalCode.R")
```

# Including an R package

If you want to include any R package that is not available out of the box in ML Studio, then you can ZIP the package and upload it. Usually, R packages are available as downloadable ZIP files. If you have already downloaded and extracted the R package that you are using in your code, you will need to ZIP the package again otherwise upload the original ZIP file for the R package to ML Studio. You need to install the R package as part of the custom code in the **Execute R Script** module and the package will be installed only for your experiment.

# Understanding the Create R Model module

The **Create R Model** module can be used to create an untrained model using R code. You can build your model using any learner based on an R package or your new implementation.

The module takes the training script and the scoring script, the two user-defined R scripts, as inputs in the property sections based on which, the model will be built.

After you create the model, you can use the **Train Model** module to train the model on a dataset similar to any other learner in ML Studio. Then, pass it to the **Score Model** module to use the model to make predictions. You can then save the trained model, create a scoring experiment, and publish it as a web service.

# Do it yourself – R

Let's take a look at the following steps to build our own test using R for coding:

1. Add another column to the data frame (in the preceding example) to move the median and plot it as another line.

    Use the moving window function `rollmedian`.

2. Display all the already installed packages in ML Studio. You may use the following code:

```
data.set <- data.frame(installed.packages())
maml.mapOutputPort("data.set")
```

# Summary

You just completed a very important part of ML Studio in this chapter. You started with an introduction to both R and Python in relation to Azure ML. You explored the importance of why you may need to extend your experiment inside ML Studio using code. Then, you learned how to execute Python scripts and import an already built code inside ML Studio. You applied the same through an example of a simple time series analysis and also created visualization with Python. After Python, you explored the same for R and performed the same tasks of time series analysis and plotted the graph with an R script. ML Studio also comes with another module to build a complete model with R apart from just running a script.

In the next chapter, you will find out how to deploy a model as a web service API from your experiment inside ML Studio, which can be consumed outside.

# 11
# Publishing a Model as a Web Service

So far, you have explored how to build different predictive models as experiments. Now, you might be wondering how that would be of use in real-life scenarios. One use of it is after you build and test your model, you can take a dataset and make a prediction straightaway inside the experiment, but in most of the cases, the result or the predictions of a model need to be used elsewhere and probably by some other people. Consider you have built a recommender model and it recommends items that a buyer might be interested in. So, these predictions require that the e-commerce site display the recommended product items to the prospective buyers. Consider one more scenario, where you have built a model for market segmentation using clustering. The marketing executive of your company should use this model for analysis by integrating the results in their software or simply by using the familiar Microsoft Excel.

Basically, you have to make the predictive model you have built available in an environment, so that people inside or outside your organization can use it. Traditionally, it used to be a cumbersome job, where a bunch of code had to be written and tested. Then, infrastructure had to be made ready as required.

Now, Azure ML takes all the pain out. In this chapter, you will explore, how easily you can publish a model in an experiment and make it available as a web service API for others to consume.

In a nutshell, you can publish your model in the following simple steps:

1. Prepare your model to be published as a web service.
2. Prepare a scoring experiment.
3. Specify the input and output for the web service.
4. Publish and test it as a web service.

# Preparing an experiment to be published

You need to get your experiment ready before you start deploying it. To do this you need to complete your experiments, run them successfully, and evaluate and identify the trained model to be used. For illustration, we have a simple model here that predicts the income of adults based on age, education, sex, and race. The model uses the **Two-Class Decision Forest** module to predict whether a person has an income of more than 50K or not. The details to build the experiment can be found in *Chapter 7, Classification Models*.

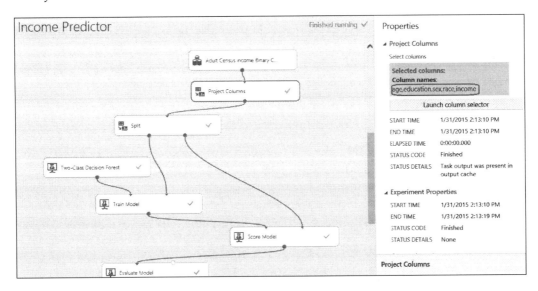

# Saving a trained model

Once you are sure about your model, you can save it as a trained model. To do this, right-click on the output port of the **Train Model** module on the canvas and then click on the **Save as Trained Model** option to save the trained model, which can be used later. You have to specify a name and the optional description text as the **Save trained model** popup appears. Then, click on the tick mark button to the right of the screen to save the trained model, as shown in the following screenshot:

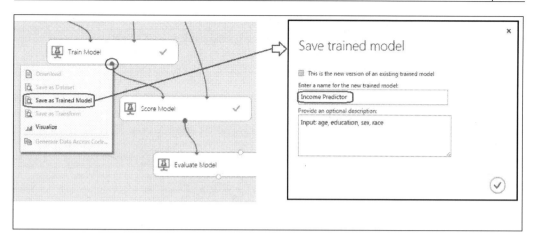

The saved model will be like a predictor module, which can be used by a **Score Model** module to score with a given feature set. It will appear as a module on the left-hand side of the screen in the module palette under the **Trained Models** group.

If you have made any changes to the model say, you've changed the parameters to the algorithm, and so on, then you have to save the trained model again, and as the popup appears, tick the **This is the new version of an existing trained model** option at the top of the screen and choose the name of the previously saved model.

# Creating a scoring experiment

A **scoring experiment** is one where you use a trained model module to make a prediction (scoring). You can create a new experiment, use a **Trained Model** module, and make a prediction with a dataset. ML Studio makes it really easy for you with a single button, as you can see in the following screenshot:

The button becomes active when the training experiment is run successfully. Run your **Income Predictor** experiment successfully and then click on the **CREATE SCORING EXPERIMENT** button to create a scoring experiment corresponding to the existing one. After this is done, you will see the following screenshot:

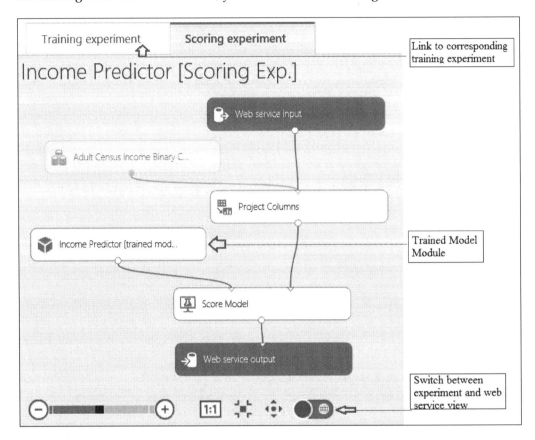

Behind the scenes, ML Studio has done the following tasks for you:

1.  It saved your trained model as a module in the **Trained Models** section of the module palette to the left of the screen.

2.  It created a copy of the existing training experiment then replaced the machine learning algorithm module and the **Train Model** module with the saved trained model.

3.  It removed the modules that were clearly not needed in a scoring experiment—the **Split** and **Evaluate Model** modules in this case.

4.  It added the **Web service input** and **Web service output** modules and connected them to the default locations in the experiment.

You can also do these steps by yourself manually and create a scoring experiment. However, by creating the experiment this way, ML Studio links up the training and scoring experiment. When you open any one link, the other will be present as a tab so that you can switch between training and scoring your experiment easily.

The **Web service input** and the **Web service output** modules specify where the input goes into and where the output comes from when the model is published as a web service. Now that these modules are connected to the default position, you need to plan and connect these to the right modules.

# Specifying the input and output of the web service

Before publishing a web service, you need to specify what the web service will take as an input and which output you are interested in. Assume that for our illustration, we need to predict a level of someone's income (that is, less than or equal to 50K or greater than or equal to 50K) from the input: age, education, sex, and race. You can achieve this using the **Project Columns** module.

In your web service, the input should go to the **Score Model** module. So, connect the **Web service input** module to the **Score Model** module. Add a **Project Columns** module and connect its input port to the output of the **Score Model** module. In the properties panel of the module, select the **Scored Labels** option only. Let's take a look at the following screenshot:

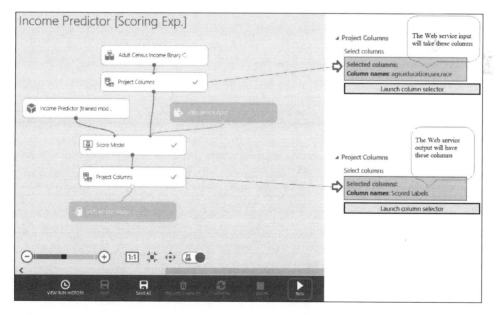

After running the experiment successfully, you can check the output of the two **Project Columns** modules in your scoring experiment; the output of which are as expected. Now, this experiment is ready to be published as a web service.

# Publishing a model as a web service

Publishing a model as a web service is very easy. To publish the model, click on the **PUBLISH WEB SERVICE** button and click on **YES** when it asks for confirmation, as shown in the following screenshot:

It may take a while and once this is done, it would take you to the published web service dashboard page. You can get back to the parent scoring experiment by clicking on the link, which is the **View latest** option (refer to **2** in the following figure). The **View snapshot** link also takes you to the same parent scoring experiment, but it shows the experiment in a locked view.

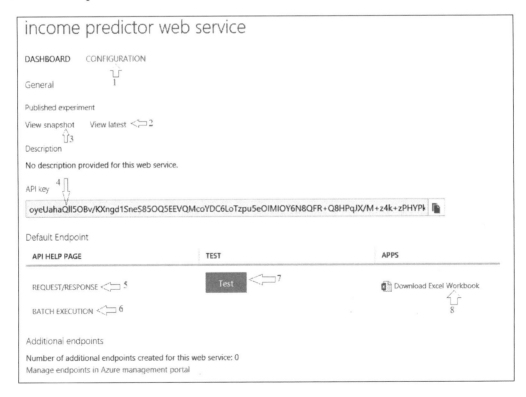

The default endpoint or the published web service API suggests how the web service would be called or consumed. The **Request/Response** option (refer to **5** in the preceding figure) specifies that you would call the web service with one feature set and get a response as a prediction based on how you defined the output. The **Batch Execution** option (refer to **6** in the preceding figure) requires that you pass a dataset (a feature matrix) as a file and get the output prediction also as a dataset.

# Visually testing a web service

You can visually test the published web service by clicking on the **Test** button (refer to **7** in the preceding figure). Click on the button and a popup form appears. Fill up the different features to make a prediction. Fill the form and click on the button with the tick mark in the bottom-right corner of the screen, as shown in the following screenshot:

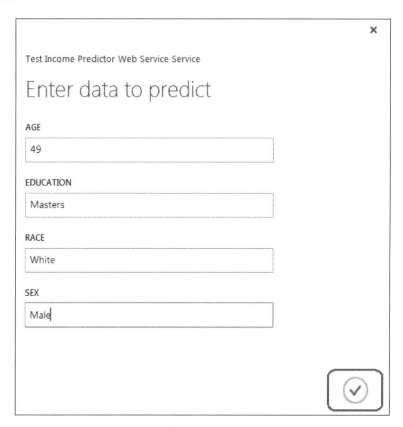

After it gets a response from the web service, you would see a message, as shown in the following figure:

As you can see in the preceding figure, it returned the predicted label "**>50K**". You can also test the web service by downloading the Excel file (refer to **8**), which is already configured to get connected with the web service. Just fill the fields to see the result.

# Consuming a published web service

Now that the web service has been published and is available as an API, you can write a program in the language of your choice and consume the API to get a prediction or the result of the API. The API needs an **API key**, which you can find on the published web service dashboard page (refer to **4**). Without the API key, you won't be able to connect to the web service. On the API help page, you will find the detailed documentation on the published API, including the sample code in **C#.Net**, **Python**, and **R**, which include the necessary inline comments. You can find the links to the API help page from the same web service dashboard page (refer to **5** and **6**).

# Web service configuration

After you publish a model, the web service name will be available on the web services page with a link to the dashboard page of the web service, as shown in the following figure:

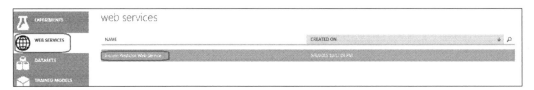

Click on the name of the web service and on the dashboard page, click on the **CONFIGURATION** option (refer to **1**). On the configuration page, you can customize the information related to the web service, for example, **Display Name**, **Description**, **Input Schema**, **Output Schema**, and so on.

# Updating the web service

You might need to update your published web service under the following two scenarios:

- Your original model changed, for example, you modified the model parameters to improve performance and so on

- You need to make changes to the input or output of the web service

For the first case, you need to go back to your original training experiment, make the changes, run it, and then click on the **UPDATE SCORING EXPERIMENT** link to update the scoring experiment. For both the scenarios, you have to go to the scoring experiment and publish it again, so it would overwrite the previously published experiment.

# Summary

In this chapter, you explored the complete steps to publish a model as a web service, so that others can use the API and consume the web service. You prepared an experiment to make it ready to be published and saved a trained model. You then created a scoring experiment and prepared it to set the input and output for the web service. You published the scoring experiment as a web service and tested it visually. You also explored ways to consume the web service API and how it can be maintained over a period of time by making configuration changes and updates.

In the next chapter, you will learn to build your own model with a case study exercise by solving a regression problem.

# 12
# Case Study Exercise I

Now you already know a decent bit about Azure ML! It's time to use that knowledge to look at some real-world problems. You may not be able to solve them fully at this point, but you can certainly give it a try and come up with some kind of a working solution.

In this chapter, we will present a problem in the form of a case study and will solve it with a very simple, but end-to-end solution. Like in other chapters so far, it won't present a step-by-step guide with all the details; however, it would just provide pointers for you to solve the problem. This chapter assumes that you have successfully completed reading all the previous chapters or already know about Azure ML.

## Problem definition and scope

If you are flying somewhere, it becomes a very bizarre experience if the flight gets delayed. We can't do much in that regard, but given the historical dataset, we can predict and know well ahead whether a particular flight will get delayed or not. That's the problem we will solve as a case study.

The complete solution to the problem of predicting a flight delay will be huge and is beyond the scope of this book because of the huge data crunching that it takes. However, we will limit the scope by limiting the dataset and simplifying the solution.

## The dataset

We will use the sample dataset that comes by default in ML Studio. This is the subset of the passenger flight's on-time performance data taken from the **TranStats** data collection from **U.S. Department of Transportation (DOT)** (http://www.transtats. bts.gov/DL_SelectFields.asp?Table_ID=236&DB_Short_Name=On-Time).

The dataset has been preprocessed and is filtered to include only the 70 busiest airports in the continental United States for the period between April 2013 to October 2013. It contains the following columns:

- **Carrier**: This contains the code assigned by IATA and is commonly used to identify a carrier.

- **OriginAirportID** (Origin Airport's Airport ID): This is an identification number assigned by DOT to identify a unique airport.

- **DestAirportID** (Destination Airport;s Airport ID): This is an identification number assigned by DOT to identify a unique airport.

- **CRSDepTime**: This is the scheduled departure time (local time in hh:mm).

- **DepDelay**: This is the difference in minutes between the scheduled and the actual departure time. Early departures show negative numbers.

- **DepDel15** (Departure Delay Indicator): This shows a delay in the departure of a flight by 15 minutes or more (here, 1=Yes).

- **CRSArrTime**: This is the scheduled arrival time (local time in hh:mm).

- **ArrDelay**: This is the difference in minutes between the scheduled and the actual arrival time. Early arrivals show negative numbers.

- **ArrDel15** (Arrival Delay Indicator): This shows a delay in the arrival of a fight by 15 minutes or more (here, 1=Yes).

- **Cancelled**: This is the cancelled flight indicator (here, 1=Yes).

 Note that the cancelled flights have been considered as delayed and have been set as *ArrDel15 = 1*.

From our experience, we know that the flight timing often gets impacted by weather conditions, so it makes sense to collect and process the relevant weather data corresponding to the origin and destination airports. For simplicity, we will consider only the flights on time dataset here. However, you are encouraged to experiment and merge the weather dataset and prepare your dataset to build the model. There is a sample **Weather Dataset** that comes by default in ML Studio.

# Data exploration and preparation

In your experiment, drag the **Flight Delays Data** sample dataset and click on the **Visualize** option to explore the dataset. You can find that some columns have lots of missing values. You can clean the missing data using a **Clean Missing Data** module by replacing it with **MICE** as the cleaning mode.

There are certain columns, such as **DayOfWeek**, **OriginAirportID**, and **DestAirportID** which contain continuous numbers; however, they are categorical variables. So, use the **Metadata Editor** module to set them as **Categorical**.

# Feature selection

Before you start developing the model, it is important to select or generate a set of variables that have the most predictive power and remove any redundant and not so important features. In this case, all the data points are of the same year, so the year column is not required here. We are interested in predicting the delays before the journey starts, so the **DepDel15** and **DepDelay** columns are not important. Again, both the **ArrDelay** and **ArrDelay15** columns are about arrival delay. Here, we are just interested in whether the flight got delayed or not. So, **ArrDelay** is not required. All the cancelled flights are labeled as delayed, so the **Cancelled** column is also not required. You filter these columns using the **Project Columns** module and you will be left with the columns that contain the required features and label.

# Model development

You have to predict whether the flight would be delayed or not. As you found from the dataset, any flight delayed for more than 15 minutes has been labeled as delayed and the **ArrDelay15** corresponding label contains 1. Here, the **ArrDelay15** column is the target variable and it only contains **0** and **1**. Clearly, it's a two-class classification problem.

As you have already explored, there are several two-class classification algorithms available in ML Studio. For simplicity, we would just build the model here with the **Two-Class Boosted Decision Tree** module with the following parameters:

- The **Maximum number of leaves per tree** option is set at **128**
- The **Minimum number of samples per leaf node** option is set at **50**
- The **Learning rate** option is set at **0.2**
- The **Number of trees constructed** option is set at **500**

You are encouraged to try out different algorithms and also use the **Sweep Parameters** module to choose the optimum parameters.

To train the model, you need to split the dataset and use one subset for training and other for scoring and evaluation.

Your experiment, after running successfully, may look something like the following:

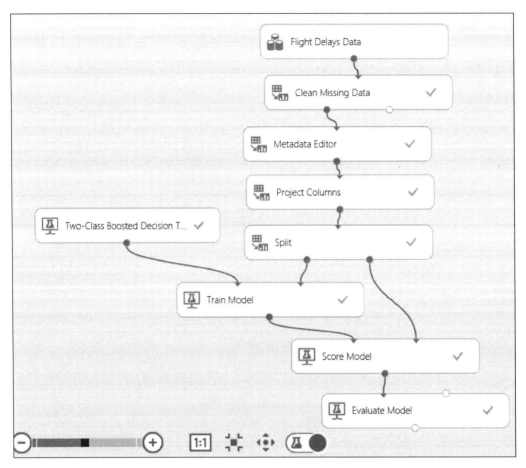

After you are happy with your experiment and satisfied with the trained model, you can proceed to deploy it by publishing it as a web service.

# Model deployment

Before publishing your model as a web service, create a scoring experiment and make sure that the **Web service input** and the **Web service output** modules are properly connected. Also, process the model if you want your output in a proper format, for example, outputting only the scored label and input to the score model may not contain the label column; in this case, you can also filter the **ArrDelay15** column along with the others in the **Project Columns** module connected to the **Score Model** module. Let's take a look at the following screenshot:

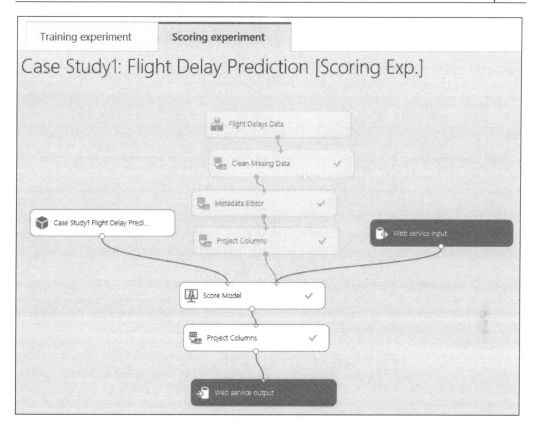

Then, publish your scoring experiment, so that it would be available as a web service in the staging environment. Test your web service visually and also with Excel. If you are good at programming, you're encouraged to test your web service by writing a small client program as well.

# Summary

You just finished building a predictive solution in this case study. You started the chapter by defining and understanding the problem. You acquired the dataset, which in this case is the sample dataset available in ML Studio. Then, you proceeded to perform data exploration and preparation before building the predictive model. You used the boosted decision tree to build the model. After running the experiment successfully, you created a scoring experiment and used a saved trained model in it. Finally, you published the experiment as a web service and tested it.

In the next chapter, you are going to learn to build your own models, with another case study where you would solve a regression problem.

# 13
# Case Study Exercise II

You already solved a real-world classification problem in the previous chapter. In this chapter, we will present a new problem in the form of another case study exercise and we will solve it with a very simple solution. This exercise represents a regression problem.

Like in the previous chapter, it won't present a step-by-step guide with all the details; however, it will provide pointers so that you can solve the problem. This chapter assumes that you have successfully completed all the previous chapters, or already know about Azure ML.

## Problem definition and scope

The problem is taken from one of the **Kaggle** machine learning competitions, where they exposed the datasets with a bit of information and asked the contestants to make a prediction from a test dataset using machine learning techniques. It is about the **Africa Soil Property Prediction Challenge**. The training dataset contains different measurements of the soil and it is expected that the contestants are able to predict values for five properties of the soil (target variables): **SOC, pH, Ca, P,** and **Sand**. Full details regarding this can be found at `https://www.kaggle.com/c/afsis-soil-properties/`.

For the purpose of this case study, we will choose just one target variable named P and ignore the others. Once you are able to predict one target variable, you can follow the same approach and predict others. So, you should try predicting all the variables by yourself.

# The dataset

You can download the dataset and find the description at `https://www.kaggle.com/c/afsis-soil-properties/data`.

The dataset has been explained in the following term list, as found at the preceding web link:

- **PIDN**: This is the unique soil sample identifier.

- **SOC**: This refers to soil organic carbon.

- **pH**: These are the pH values.

- **Ca**: This is the Mehlich-3 extractable calcium.

- **P**: This is the Mehlich-3 extractable phosphorus.

- **Sand**: This is the sand content.

- **m7497.96 - m599.76**: There are 3,578 mid-infrared absorbance measurements. For example, the "m7497.96" column is the absorbance at wavenumber 7497.96 cm-1. We suggest you remove spectra CO2 bands, which are in the region m2379.76 to m2352.76, but you do not have to.

- **Depth**: This is the depth of the soil sample (this has two categories: "**Topsoil**" and "**Subsoil**"). They have also included some potential spatial predictors from remote sensing data sources. Short variable descriptions of different terms are provided below and additional descriptions can be found in AfSIS data. The data has been mean centered and scaled.

- **BSA**: These are the average long-term **Black Sky Albedo** measurements from the **MODIS** satellite images (here, BSAN = near-infrared, BSAS = shortwave, and BSAV = visible).

- **CTI**: This refers to the **Compound Topographic Index** calculated from the **Shuttle Radar Topography Mission** elevation data.

- **ELEV**: This refers to the Shuttle Radar Topography Mission elevation data.

- **EVI**: This is the average long-term **Enhanced Vegetation Index** from the MODIS satellite images.

- **LST**: This is the average long-term **Land Surface Temperatures** from the MODIS satellite images (here, LSTD = day time temperature and LSTN = night time temperature).

- **Ref**: This refers to the average long-term **Reflectance** measurements from the MODIS satellite images (here, Ref1 = blue, Ref2 = red, Ref3 = near-infrared, and Ref7 = mid-infrared).

- **Reli**: This is the topographic **Relief** calculated from the Shuttle Radar Topography mission elevation data.

- **TMAP and TMFI**: These refer to the average long-term **Tropical Rainfall Monitoring Mission** data (here, TMAP = mean annual precipitation and TMFI = modified fournier index).

Download the training dataset (`https://www.kaggle.com/c/afsis-soil-properties/download/train.zip`). Note that you may have to create an account to download the dataset. Upload the dataset to ML Studio (for this, refer to *Chapter 4, Getting Data in and out of ML Studio*, to find details on how to upload a dataset from your local machine to ML Studio).

# Data exploration and preparation

Create a new experiment in ML Studio. Drag the uploaded dataset to the canvas and visualize it. As you can see, it has 1157 rows and 3600 columns. Usually, the data exposed in a Kaggle competition is already cleaned, which saves you the effort of data cleansing, such as dealing with missing values. In ML Studio, you can't see all the columns and rows. There are 3,578 columns that have mid-infrared absorbance measurements and these entire column names start with the letter 'm'. You may like to separate them out. To do so, you can use an **Execute Python Script** module with the following code, where the inline comments explain the lines of code. For this, refer to *Chapter 10, Extensibility with R and Python*, to find the details on how to integrate a Python/R script inside ML Studio:

```python
def azureml_main(dataframe1 = None, dataframe2 = None):
    #Get all the columns
    cols = dataframe1.columns.tolist()
    #Select columns with name starting with letter 'm'
    dataframe1=dataframe1[[col for col in cols if
col.startswith('m')]]
    #Return the modified dataset
    return dataframe1
```

The model in progress may appear as follows:

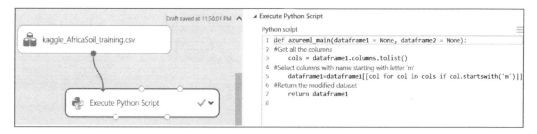

Alternatively, you can also use an **Execute R Script** module with R code to achieve the same.

These extracted 3,578 columns are almost impossible to visualize and will take a long time to process in a model, especially when you use the **Sweep Parameters** module. It would be worthwhile condensing them into a few lines, so they are easier to process. The **Principal Component Analysis** module would be of great help, as it would extract a given number of the most relevant features from the given features. The **Principal Component Analysis** (PCA) is a popular technique that takes a feature set and computes a new feature set with reduced dimensionality or a lesser number of features or components; with most of the information contained in the original feature set. The **Principal Component Analysis** module present in ML Studio takes **Number of dimensions to reduce to** as input, where you can specify the desired, low number of features.

You may try **10** components (for the **Number of dimensions to reduce to** option) as its parameter, as shown in the following figure:

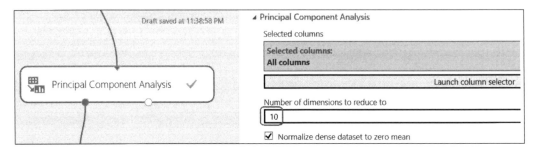

You may use another **Execute Python Script** module or **Execute R Script** to extract other relevant columns, which are all the columns excluding those that start with 'm' and other target variables (because we are only interested in P). You may also like to exclude PIDN, which is the unique soil sample identifier. Let's take a look at the following screenshot:

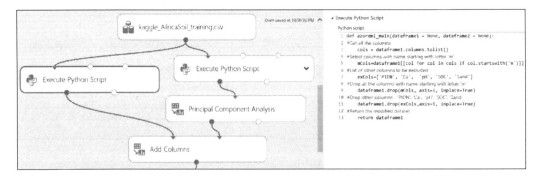

The Python code for the same is as follows:

```
def azureml_main(dataframe1 = None, dataframe2 = None):
    #Get all the columns
    cols = dataframe1.columns.tolist()
    #Select columns with name starting with letter 'm'
    mCols=dataframe1[[col for col in cols if col.startswith('m')]]
    #List of other columns to be excluded
    exCols=['PIDN', 'Ca', 'pH', 'SOC', 'Sand']
    #Drop all the columns with name starting with letter 'm'
    dataframe1.drop(mCols, axis=1, inplace=True)
    #Drop other columns - 'PIDN', 'Ca', 'pH', 'SOC', 'Sand'
    dataframe1.drop(exCols,axis=1, inplace=True)
    #Return the modified dataset
    return dataframe1
```

Use the two sets of extracted columns to combine, and make, one dataset using the **Add Columns** module. By now, you should have a reduced feature set, but you still have to find the most relevant ones. Unnecessary data or noise may reduce the predictive power of a model, so should be excluded. The **Filter Based Feature Selection** module can identify the most important features in a dataset. You may try the same with a different number of desired features as parameters, and evaluate the performance of the overall model.

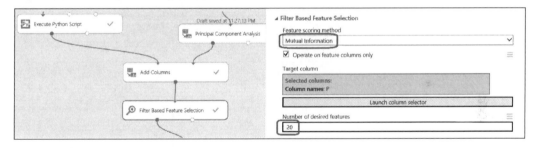

Before you proceed in building the model, you need to prepare train, validate, and test dataset. Let's take a look at the following screenshot:

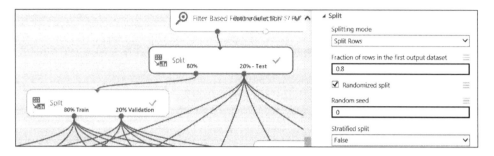

# Model development

After preparing your data, you are not sure which model or regression algorithm would perform well for the problem at hand. Because the target variable P is continuous, you know that it's a regression problem. So, it would be worthwhile trying different algorithms and choosing the best one. You may use the **Sweep Parameters** module to obtain the optimum parameters for the algorithm. You need to pass three inputs to the **Sweep Parameters** module: the untrained algorithm, training dataset, and validation dataset. Use the **Score** modules to score the test data. Use an **Evaluate** module to compare the two models with the scored data.

You should try different algorithms to choose the best one. The following figure is just for your reference, which shows four algorithms.

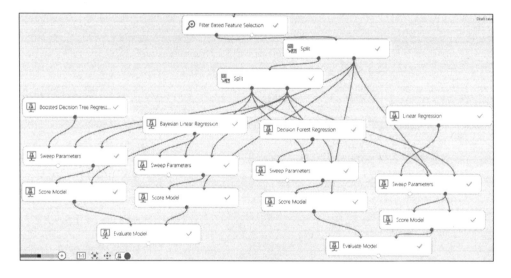

Run the model and find out which algorithm performs the best for you.

# Model deployment

After you are happy with a particular model, save it as a trained model and then prepare an experiment for a web service and proceed to deploy the model. Refer to *Chapter 11, Publishing a Model as a Web Service*, to find the details on how to deploy a model to the staging environment and test it visually in ML Studio.

# Summary

In this last chapter, you solved another real-world problem. You started with understanding the problem and then, acquired the necessary data. After initial data exploration, you realized that the data has a large number of columns, so you used Python script modules to first split the data into two sets of features, and then used the PCA algorithm to get a reduced set of features. Then, you used the **Filter Based Feature Selection** module, which can identify most of the important features from the reduced dataset. To select the right model, you tried different algorithms and trained them with optimum parameters using the **Sweep Parameters** modules. Finally, you selected the model and proceeded to publish it as a web service.

# Index

Fisher Linear Discriminant Analysis
    module 67
outliers, removing 63, 64
**Data Reader module, ML Studio 48**
**dataset**
  about 26, 165
  Black Sky Albedo (BSA) 172
  Ca 172
  columns 166
  Compound Topographic Index (CTI) 172
  ELEV 172
  EVI 172
  Land Surface Temperatures (LST) 172
  m7497.96 - m599.76 172
  P 172
  pH 172
  PIDN 172
  Ref 172
  Reli 172
  Sand 172
  SOC 172
  soil, depth 172
  TMAP 173
  TMFI 173
  URL 75, 172
**data, splitting**
  Recommender Split 61
  Regular Expression 61
  Relative Expression 62
**decision forest regression 82-84**
**decision-tree-based models**
  about 7
  used, for predicting adult income 104-109
**deep learning algorithms 7**
**determination**
  coefficient 74
**diabetes**
  classifying 97

# E

**Energy Efficiency Regression data**
  **module 44**
**Enter Data module, ML Studio 47**

**ETL (Extract, Transform, and Load) 2**
**evaluate algorithm 70**
**evaluate model 86**
**evaluate recommender 135**
**evaluation metrics, classification**
  about 92
  accuracy 93
  Area Under the Curve (AUC) 95
  F1 score 94
  false negative 93
  false positive 92
  matric 96
  precision 94
  recall 94
  receiver operating characteristics
    (ROC) graph 95
  threshold 94
  true negative 93
  true positive 92
**Execute Python Script module 143-145**
**Execute R Script module 149, 150**
**experiment**
  preparing, to publish 156

# F

**F1 score 94**
**Filter Based Feature Selection module 66**
**Fisher Linear Discriminant Analysis**
  **module 67**
**Full Outer Join 60**

# H

**histogram 29, 30**
**Hive Table 45**

# I

**Inner Join 60**
**Iris dataset**
  multiclass classification with 111, 112
  URL 111, 112
**issue**
  scope 165

modules
  evaluating 97
  scoring 97
  training 97
multiclass classification
  about 110
  evaluation metrics 111
  with Iris dataset 111
  with Wine dataset 118
multiclass classification, with Iris dataset
  about 111, 112
  models, comparing 115-118
  multiclass decision forest 112-115
multiclass classification, with Wine dataset
  about 118
  multiclass neural network, with
      parameter sweep 119, 120
Multiple Imputation by Chained
      Equations (MICE) 56

# N

neural network
  about 7
  and boosted decision tree, comparing 86-88
No free lunch theorem 89

# O

Ordinal Regression Model 88
outliers
  about 32
  removing 63, 64

# P

parameters
  optimizing, for learner 80, 81
parameter sweeping
  multiclass neural network with 119, 120
  Two-class neural network 102-104
predictive analytics
  about 1, 2
  data, collecting 2
  data, exploring 3
  issue, defining 2
  issue, scope 2

model, deploying 3
model, developing 3
Principal Component
      Analysis (PCA) 56, 174
Python
  about 142
  code, extending 142, 143
  existing code, importing 148
  used, for creating visualizations 146
Python script
  time series analysis, performing
      with 146-148

# R

R
  about 142
  code, importing 152
  Execute R Script module 149, 150
  extending 142, 143
  time series analysis 150, 151
  used, for extending experiments 149
receiver operating characteristics
      (ROC) graph 95
regression algorithms
  about 69, 70
  Bayesian Linear Regression Model 88
  Ordinal Regression Model 88
  Poisson Regression 88
regression issue, machine learning 6
relative absolute error (RAE) 73
relative squared error (RSE) 73, 74
root mean squared error (RMSE) 73
R package
  including 152

# S

scatter plot 32, 33
score algorithm 70
score matchbox recommender 134
scoring experiment
  creating 157-159
SQL Azure Tables 49
standard deviation 28, 29
Supervised Machine Learning 4
SVMLight 45
sweep parameters module 80, 81

## Thank you for buying
# Microsoft Azure Machine Learning

# About Packt Publishing

Packt, pronounced 'packed', published its first book, *Mastering phpMyAdmin for Effective MySQL Management*, in April 2004, and subsequently continued to specialize in publishing highly focused books on specific technologies and solutions.

Our books and publications share the experiences of your fellow IT professionals in adapting and customizing today's systems, applications, and frameworks. Our solution-based books give you the knowledge and power to customize the software and technologies you're using to get the job done. Packt books are more specific and less general than the IT books you have seen in the past. Our unique business model allows us to bring you more focused information, giving you more of what you need to know, and less of what you don't.

Packt is a modern yet unique publishing company that focuses on producing quality, cutting-edge books for communities of developers, administrators, and newbies alike. For more information, please visit our website at www.packtpub.com.

# About Packt Enterprise

In 2010, Packt launched two new brands, Packt Enterprise and Packt Open Source, in order to continue its focus on specialization. This book is part of the Packt Enterprise brand, home to books published on enterprise software – software created by major vendors, including (but not limited to) IBM, Microsoft, and Oracle, often for use in other corporations. Its titles will offer information relevant to a range of users of this software, including administrators, developers, architects, and end users.

# Writing for Packt

We welcome all inquiries from people who are interested in authoring. Book proposals should be sent to author@packtpub.com. If your book idea is still at an early stage and you would like to discuss it first before writing a formal book proposal, then please contact us; one of our commissioning editors will get in touch with you.

We're not just looking for published authors; if you have strong technical skills but no writing experience, our experienced editors can help you develop a writing career, or simply get some additional reward for your expertise.

# R Machine Learning Essentials

ISBN: 978-1-78398-774-0          Paperback: 218 pages

Gain quick access to the machine learning concepts and practical applications using the R development environment

1. Build machine learning algorithms using the most powerful tools in R.

2. Identify business problems and solve them by developing effective solutions.

3. Hands-on tutorial explaining the concepts through lots of practical examples, tips and tricks.

# Mastering Machine Learning with scikit-learn

ISBN: 978-1-78398-836-5          Paperback: 238 pages

Apply effective learning algorithms to real-world problems using scikit-learn

1. Design and troubleshoot machine learning systems for common tasks including regression, classification, and clustering.

2. Acquaint yourself with popular machine learning algorithms, including decision trees, logistic regression, and support vector machines.

3. A practical example-based guide to help you gain expertise in implementing and evaluating machine learning systems using scikit-learn.

# Clojure for Machine Learning

ISBN: 978-1-78328-435-1    Paperback: 292 pages

Successfully leverage advanced machine learning techniques using the Clojure ecosystem

1. Covers a lot of machine learning techniques with Clojure programming.

2. Encompasses precise patterns in data to predict future outcomes using various machine learning techniques.

3. Packed with several machine learning libraries available in the Clojure ecosystem.

# Machine Learning with R

ISBN: 978-1-78216-214-8    Paperback: 396 pages

Learn how to use R to apply powerful machine learning methods and gain an insight into real-world applications

1. Harness the power of R for statistical computing and data science.

2. Use R to apply common machine learning algorithms with real-world applications.

3. Prepare, examine, and visualize data for analysis.

4. Understand how to choose between machine learning models.

Please check **www.PacktPub.com** for information on our titles

74567722R00119

Made in the USA
Middletown, DE
27 May 2018